BEYOND THE FRONTIER

Camp Lectures 1981

BEYOND THE FRONTIER

The politics of a failed mission; Bulgaria 1944

E.P. Thompson

Stanford University Press
Stanford, California
1997

Stanford University Press

Stanford California

©1997 Dorothy Thompson

Originating publisher: The Merlin Press, Suffolk

First published in U.S.A. by

Stanford University Press, 1997

Printed in Finland

Cloth ISBN 0-8047-2896-8

Paper ISBN 0-8047-2897-6

LC 96-70260

This book is printed on acid-free paper

As one, who, gazing at a vista
  Of beauty, sees the clouds close in
And turns his back in sorrow, hearing
  The Thunderclaps begin

So we, whose life was all before us,
  Our hearts with sunlight filled,
Left in the hills our books and flowers,
  Descended, and were killed

Write on the stone no words of sadness,
  - Only the gladness due
That we, who asked the most of living,
  Knew how to give it too.

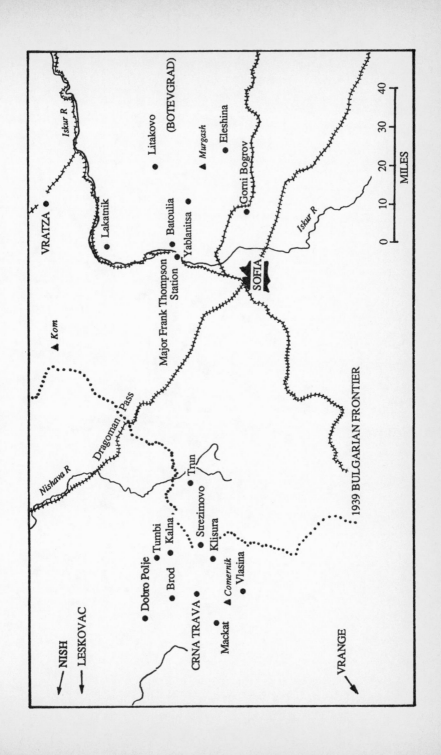

NISH →
LESKOVAC →

Nishava R

Dragoman Pass

Iskur R

VRATZA ●

Lakatnik ●

▲ *Kom*

Iskar R

CRNA TRAVA ●

Dobro Polje ●

Tumbi ●
Brod ● Kalna ●

Trun ●

Strezimovo ●
Klisura ●

Mackat ●
▲ *Comernik*
Vlasina ●

1939 BULGARIAN FRONTIER

VRANGE →

SOFIA

Major Frank Thompson
Station

Batoulia ●
Yablanitsa ●

Litakovo ●
(BOTEVGRAD)

▲ *Murgash*
Eleshina ●

Gorni Bogrov ●

MILES
0   10   20   30   40

Acknowledgements

ALTHOUGH I helped in the preparation of these lectures, my work was mainly on the official records. I was not always in touch with the many contacts Edward made with friends and associates of his brother; their reminiscences are an essential element in the lectures and I hope that I have mentioned all those who helped. If any have been omitted please forgive me.

Particular thanks must go to Iris Murdoch who is a constant presence in the story and whose letters from Frank are the most intimate and revealing. Quotations from her poem *The Agamemnon Class, 1939* are printed with her permission. Lord Henniker who was one of the last British army officers to see Frank before he went into Bulgaria has been generous with his time and his memories; Freeman Dyson, Michael Foot, Tony Foster and Leo Platsky have all contributed sympathetic memories; the late Hugh Seton-Watson in correspondence and in conversations gave Edward information and clarification which was of considerable help. Peter Wright has given us a very interesting account of his meeting with Frank in the Middle East in 1942 and 1943 which it has not been possible to incorporate with the present text, but which will help to build up the fuller picture which I hope will one day be written. The late Elizabeth Barker was helpful in every way and some of the most valuable discussions in the preparation of the project took place in her house. Basil Davidson, whose

1

own experience as a British liaison officer is part of the history of the war in this sector, has been a constant source of advice and help as well as representing in his own life and work the values for which Frank Thompson fought.

In Bulgaria most of the information we received was anecdotal and of dubious value but we were aided by a group of young historians who helped us to obtain rare printed sources and by the film makers, particularly by Slavcho Trunski, in 1979 a general with a slightly hazy memory of the war years, but one whose own partisan experience helped us to understand more of the setting of the story.

The late Stowers Johnson provided his own account in his book, and was also very helpful in correspondence and conversations which went beyond what he was able to publish.

Simon Kusseff is working on a larger work about Frank Thompson and his friends; he has gone meticulously through Frank's papers and has been most helpful in sorting and arranging the material. He has also given a lot of help in other ways, in corresponding with people whose testimony Edward used in the lectures, and in helping to arrange a contribution on Frank Thompson for the one-day seminar on Anglo-Bulgarian relations which was held in the House of Commons on the 18th May 1995.

Marietta Stankova has given valuable advice and help in the regularisation of the spelling of Bulgarian names and places. These occur in different forms in various documents and printed sources.

Martin Eve has overseen the reconstruction work on the lectures from the beginning and has helped in numerous ways, in particular in filling in some of the background narrative in the introduction.

Transcripts of Crown-copyright records in the Public Records Office appear by permission of the Controller of H.M.Stationery Office. Our thanks for permission to quote from his book *Disturbing the Universe* to Freeman Dyson and the publisher Harper and Row, New York, and for the extract from W.H. Auden's *Poems* to Messrs Faber and Faber.

Dorothy Thompson

Introduction

IN the spring of 1978 Edward received a letter from his friend
Peter Stansky, sounding him out on the possibility of his
accepting an invitation to deliver the Camp Lectures at
Stanford University. The lectures were, Stansky explained, 'a
series of three [with] the stipulation…that they be on a topic
that would be a new area for you, and not something on which
you have already written.' The Spring of 1980 or 1981 were
suggested as dates.

In 1978 Edward had been away from full-time University
teaching for several years, and was well on his way to
finishing his major book of eighteenth century studies to
which he had already given the title *Customs in Common*. He
liked the idea of a visit to Stanford, but faced a problem with
the selection of a subject, since the commitment involved the
publication of the lectures. He wrote to the committee 'I
cannot take out any part of my study of eighteenth-century
social history which I hope to finish next year. My longer term
study of the English Romantic poets in the 1790s also presents
problems - of taking out a distinct theme - although…the
rights of women might be possible.' This latter he had
suggested in an earlier letter as the possible subject of three
lectures and a subsequent 'small book' which would take him
some time to complete after the lectures. It would be about
'the whole question of rights of women and the debate around

this in the 1790s, a question which - despite many biographies of Mary Wollstonecraft - has never been examined fully in the round...' But as he was mulling over possible areas of work, he came up with another idea -'I have now thought out a completely different possible topic' he wrote to the chairman of the committee, having by now accepted the invitation in principle '...one in which I have no claim to expertise, except personal participation: i.e. "War Memoirs". I don't, of course, mean my memories of the Battle of Cassino. I mean that, as far as my knowledge goes, there are things about the years 1939-48 [sic] which 'my' generation have been reticent about and have never bothered to try to explain to the beastly young...'

The original idea for the lectures would have involved many different types of experience and recollection. They would be 'in no known discipline, but would combine literary history and criticism, social history and politics and a little reminiscence: they would be heavily English in background, but the final lecture would end (with poetry) in California...' The proposal at that stage was 'still only half-formed', but out of it came his idea to return to a question which had been on his mind since the war years, the death of his older brother Frank as a British Liaison Officer with the Bulgarian partisans in 1944. He had done as much research as was possible in the immediate[*] post-war years, and now saw the opportunity to re-examine the history, making use of sources which were becoming available, but also looking at the way a particular episode had been recorded and expounded in the years since the war. It was to be the examination of 'war reminiscences'

*   E.P. Thompson and T.J. Thompson, *There is a Spirit in Europe* Gollancz 1947, and esp. 2nd edition, 1948.

5

as they concerned one particular event. The narrowing down of the original subject occurred for a variety of reasons.

The Bulgarian events of 1944 had been brought back into the foreground of Edward's memory partly by the publication in 1975 of Stowers Johnson's *Agents Extraordinary*, which was clearly based on recent visits to Bulgaria and interviews with participants, but even more by the visit to our house in Worcestershire in the summer of 1977 of a Bulgarian film director and crew. Slavcho Trunsky, who appears quite a lot in the following pages, came with his wife, an experienced film-maker, and a crew of half a dozen or so technicians to make a film about Frank's life to be shown to English-speaking audiences. They stayed a couple of days and we were able to talk at length on many subjects. When we told them that we had 'lost touch with Bulgaria' after 1948, Madame Trunski replied with a wry smile, 'We nearly lost touch with Bulgaria at that time too.' It seemed as though many of the former partisans were now accessible, and the possibility of meeting them, especially Dencho Znepolski, whom he had met in 1947 and who had played so important a part in the story of the Second Sofia Brigade, made Edward decide to visit Bulgaria. It was by then possible to travel as ordinary tourists, and we told Slavcho that we would come on our own, with our own car, paying our own way. We did not want to be guests of the government or of any official body, although we would welcome help in contacting any survivors of the war years from whom we could gain fresh information.

Edward and I rarely worked togther on historical projects, although we always read and discussed each others' work. On the Bulgarian project, however, we did cooperate to some degree, since it was necessary to work quickly once we had decided on the Bulgarian visit. He made contact with a number of other historians who had worked on the war in the Balkans, including Elizabeth Barker whose *British Policy in South-East*

Europe in the Second World War had been published in 1976. Both the book and Miss Barker herself provided invaluable guidance through the official records. We worked together on the infuriatingly weeded War Office and Foreign Office and other government papers, and by the time we actually visited Bulgaria in the spring of 1979 we had a pretty good idea of what information was now available and what we were looking for in our Bulgarian travels. In the event, after a very valuable short stay in Yugoslavia where we were able to visit many of the areas in which the early days of the partisan brigade were spent, and where we were able to move around as we liked and to meet and speak to old people including some of the former partisans, we arrived in Sofia, only to be hijacked by the representatives of the government, including General Trunski, and subjected to a very full official programme, some of which is described in these lectures.

By the summer of 1979 Edward was fully engaged in the research and in beginning to write up the material. But by the winter of that year history caught up with him, and the proposal to site cruise missiles in western and southern Europe led to the campaign of resistance in which most of his last years were spent. When he went to Stanford in 1981 he was very conscious of the inadequacy of the preparation for the lectures. He began the first with an apology:

> In the past eighteen months I have been so fully preoccupied with matters which concern me as a citizen - the settled direction towards a terminal nuclear collision in Europe - that I have had to set aside for a time my work as a historian. I have been forced to leave libraries and to spend my time in public meetings and to turn my pen to pamphlets and public correspondence... I accepted your generous invitation with pleasure more than two years ago, in all innocence; it was beyond the foreknowledge of your committee, or of myself, that in the interval Russian troops would enter Afghanistan,

NATO would proceed to implant cruise missiles in my country, Polish Solidarity would arise and flourish, that new military and strategic advisers would arise to dominance in the United States and that my own continent of Europe would draw its breath in the expectation of being the site of a 'theatre' nuclear war. And that, for reasons connected with all these things, I should find myself standing here, unable to present to you either new historical research or theoretical conceptions of an adequacy of presentation to meet this occasion.

His apology was for the restriction of his subject to a single set of events rather than to the wider issues he had originally envisaged. He introduced his account of his brother's war experience and death by offering it as an example of the many different ways in which one event can be used, and also as an indication of some of the many problems involved in any kind of historical narrative. It was in many ways an ideal subject since it was not a major decisive episode, but was still of a high enough profile to attract the attention of historians and politicians as well as simply the interest of one family. He gave the lectures from notes, some more fully written out than others, and he always intended to fulfil his obligation to Stanford and put them in order for publication. But the peace movement and then years of ill-health intervened, and they remained in the condition in which he had set them aside in 1981. We have reproduced them as well as we could from his notes, wherever possible in his own words. We have added a few notes, mostly to locate and clarify references, but occasionally to update a little where this seemed to be helpful.

The context of the events described in the lectures will be familiar to those who lived through those years. Others may need reminding of the exact state of the war in early 1944 when Frank Thompson was parachuted into Serbia.

On the Eastern Front the Red Army had followed up the

decisive victory at Stalingrad by sweeping across the plains of the Ukraine; the British and American forces had driven the enemy from North Africa, taken Sicily and, in September, occupied the south of the Italian mainland - toppling Mussolini's fascist regime and knocking Italy out of the war. To the west the long-awaited second front was clearly going to be opened on a large scale in the Spring or early Summer.

On top of all this, the Nazis faced an increasing threat on their southern flank - in the Balkans. Partisan bands were active throughout Yugoslavia and had survived major offensives aimed at encircling and destroying them. They had captured garrison towns like Tuzla in Bosnia and had established free areas in which they could strike at enemy lines of communication. In Greece too the guerilla struggle had passed beyond the stage of harassment to the establishment of liberated zones and a structured army of 50,000 mobile troops. In both countries, and in Albania, the Italian collapse had brought the resistance armies a bonanza of modern arms and equipment. Their forces had always been short of arms, never of men.

German *blitzkrieg* had totally altered the nature of war, the trench warfare of World War I being replaced by rapid movement. This highly mobile form of warfare demanded new forms of organisation. Airborne troops and Commandos required rapid and effective systems of communication. One entirely new organisation had been set up to relay information to headquarters about the movement of their forward troops. This was the body known as Phantom in which Frank Thompson served for a time in the Middle East and in Sicily.

Another organisation that reflected the changing nature of aspects of the war was SOE. Special Operations Executive was set up by Winston Churchill when he took office as premier in 1940. Unlike the Intelligence services which owed allegiance to the Foreign Office, SOE came under the Ministry of Economic Warfare. The high degree of autonomy and of freedom from Foreign Office constraints given by this structure allowed SOE to forge ahead with its objective of 'setting Europe ablaze' - i.e. of supplying arms and other support to guerilla and sabotage groups. In more than one case such a programme could come directly into conflict with the ideas of the Foreign Office. Above all there must clearly have been a conflict between those attempting to influence neutral governments in such countries as Hungary, Bulgaria, Spain and even Italy, and those helping subversive groups to overthrow them in favour of a clear pro-allied regime. In addition, of course, the Foreign Office must always have been looking beyond the expediencies of immediate wartime engagements to possible British interests in the post-war settlements.

SOE personnel as a whole were not characterised by their conformity or their orthodoxy. Some were former Civil Servants, or even indeed bankers, like Bickham Sweet-Escott, author of *Baker Street Irregular*, a personal account of SOE; a fair number were scholars, like Frank from Winchester and New College, or C.M.Woodhouse, a Greek specialist and linguist. The wireless operators came from a different elite, highly skilled at their job, many of them NCOs from the RAF. Among the interpreters were a number of Canadians of Croatian origin who had been especially recruited for the operations. Regular army officers were the exception in SOE, although one of the best-known among the liaison officers was a regular, Colonel Myers, a sapper and the first head of the mission in Greece. Basil Davidson, whose mission to Hungary was in many ways analogous to Frank's Bulgarian assignment, later wrote a first hand account of the Yugoslav resistance in his book *Partisan Picture*. These liaison officers had to be capable of taking immediate decisions and of acting on their own initiative. They were working with men and women who had taken to the mountains to fight an invading enemy; these people were not thinking about promotion or about their next leave. The SOE teams shared their hardships and also their dedication and single-mindedness.

It is inevitable that accounts of the events in these informal theatres of war are often fragmentary or even contradictory. The problem of the recording and transmission of information was enormous. Wireless telegraphy was in its infancy, depending on heavy, bulky transmitters powered by batteries and generating equipment. These sets could be manhandled over short distances, but otherwise a mule was needed to transport them across difficult terrain, or across any but the smallest distances. Keeping the sets on the air was a skilled job and coding and decoding were essential and time-consuming. Every SOE Liaison Officer had to have a W/T operator, and these two, together with an interpreter when necessary, made up the basic team as a rule.

In preparing these lectures for publication, I have been very much aware that they represented for Edward the beginning of a work which he was never able to complete. He did not intend them as an act of family piety, nor as the celebration of the courage and sacrifice of one particular soldier. For him his brother's life illustrated the qualities which so many of the young men showed in those years, and he intended to look again at the experience of the war years and at their treatment by politicians and historians in the succeeding half century. Frank was more articulate and left more of a personal record than most of those who died, and his writing and his actions may help us to decode the experience of some at least of those who left no record.

In a similar way, the Bulgarian episode which was to a degree isolated and which involved comparatively small numbers, may help to illustrate the complexity and confusion of the years in which almost the whole of Europe was involved either actively in battle or in the opaque resistance to occupation. Modern dramas and reconstructions too easily give the impression of solid systems of command, control and communication which were simply not in place in many parts of the warring continent. SOE and other agencies operating at the frontiers of controllable activity were involved in conspiracies and in cock-ups. Some of the most successful operations began in quite as chancy a way as the events described in these pages. The interests involved and the axes being ground were by no means clear, and the variety in the accounts given of the Balkan resistance movements in the ensuing half century illustrates the way in which the politics of the Cold War and of world politics since it ended have been allowed to influence the telling of the tale and the attribution of motives to the participants.

It is clear, too, that this is the story not of one brother but of two. When Frank was in Bulgaria Edward was in Italy, soon to take part in the battle of Cassino. Many of the letters in which Frank most explicitly discussed political questions were those that he wrote to his younger brother. The extensive correspondence between them may at some time be of interest to historians concerned with the ideas of the war generation. Those of us who survived the war are now a half century away from the events described here. Historians have written about the war who were not even born when it was raging. Edward's life, like that of most of our generation, was lived with memories of the war and to some extent in the presence of those who did not survive. One of the legacies left by his older brother was a deeply-felt commitment to Europe. From their family they inherited Indian and Middle Eastern connections, and they were by birth half-American, but both brothers felt their closest affinities to be with the peoples of the European continent. Perhaps a reminder of the wartime experience of fighting alongside the ordinary citizens of Europe may still contribute to a resolution of the problems which are tearing the continent apart today.

D.T.

Lecture One

THE matter with which this series of talks deals belongs both to the present and to the past: it is historical, and yet it is not quite 'history'. It concerns an event which, in terms of public history, is trivial; marginal; meriting a footnote. I cannot ask you to share my own personal concern to establish 'the truth' of the matter. Yet, as has been shown by two distinguished authors known very well to this campus, journeys to frontiers may illuminate further intellectual and political matters, and it is my hope that this journey across a frontier may do this also. And, beyond that, there are certain questions of method, in its more technical sense, which might be illustrated. I am not so much concerned with historical epistemology - what is 'fact', what is interpretation - as with more humdrum questions: the activities of anti-historians, how sensitive evidence is destroyed or screened, how myths originate, how historical anecdote may simply be a code for ideology, how the reasons of state are eternally at war with historical knowledge. I am concerned with these humdrum questions - and certain even more technical problems of collecting oral history.

*****

Let us start with one of these. Two years ago, almost to the day, my wife and I found ourselves (somewhat to our own surprise) driving in a large black official Volga car across

14

Central Bulgaria in the company of a high-ranking officer in the Bulgarian army. This is not the normal situation in which Western academics are accustomed to find themselves, and still less persons rather well known for their opposition to Marxist orthodoxies and their commitment to civil and intellectual liberties. To explain this single circumstance would require some time, and it might offer us one theme of these lectures - the endless discrepancies between the trajectories of personal experience, of individuals, and those public trajectories of quantities, of trends, tendencies and process with which historians normally concern themselves.

As I meditated this point, our very courteous host turned to us and announced, with some complacency, through the interpreter: 'It is said that the second Sofia Partisan Brigade was defeated because the British Liaison staff were reporting daily to Cairo, and Cairo was then sending messages on to the Bulgarian authorities as to the route of the march and the daily location of the partisans.' I checked the statement back, point by point. Then, clutching at my own discipline, I asked 'Who says this? Upon what evidence?' Our host settled back comfortably in his seat, with a knowing expression: 'This is what is said. By people who know.'

But this is not all that 'people who know' have had to say about the extraordinary march of the 2nd Sofia Partisan Brigade from the Serbian frontier into the heart of Bulgaria. A few weeks before this episode I had picked up another story and this came, characteristically (for Britain), in the form of the half-drunken gossip of a former intelligence officer, relayed through a third party. It was said, in this case, that the officer commanding the British liaison unit accompanying the partisans had crossed the frontier into Bulgaria contrary to the direct orders of his superiors in Cairo. More than that, the British signals sergeant had challenged the order to advance across the frontier, and had been forced to comply by his commanding officer at pistol point. In the event, the Bulgarian partisans robbed the British party of their gold and then betrayed them into the hands of the Bulgarian authorities.

A good deal of contemporary history rests upon the information of 'people who know'. The problem is, not that they know nothing, but that they do, in fact, know a great deal. But what they know can pass, over the years, by a process of selection, into an ideological code which presents, in the form of anecdote or fact, what they wish to be believed. If, at the same time, harder evidential material is suppressed or destroyed, the truth of a past event may become irrecoverable.

To explain these two anecdotes, by 'people who know', I must first present to you the bare bones - no more than a skeletal structure - of certain events in South-East Europe in the first half of 1944. I shall return, in this and subsequent lectures, to this or that moment within these events; but this will be my only consecutive relation.

September 1943 saw significant developments in the Balkan Resistance movement. Brigadier Fitzroy Maclean was sent into Tito's partisan headquarters as Churchill's personal representative, thus signalling a decisive shift in the western allies' support for the partisans and against Mihailovich; Italian forces surrendered, and their arms in many cases fell into Yugoslav and Albanian partisan hands; a British mission entitled 'Mulligatawny', commanded by Major Mostyn Davies, was infiltrated into Albania. The objective of this Mission was to make contact with representatives of Bulgarian partisans on the Macedonian or Serbian frontier with Bulgaria. After a hazardous journey, with a small partisan escort, through territory occupied alternately by partisans, Chetniks and German occupying forces, Mulligatawny arrived some three months later in the Crna Trava area of South Serbia. On 4th January 1944 the Mission finally made contact with two representatives of the military HQ of the Fatherland Front

16

(based in Sofia) code-named Ivan and Gorsho.[1] The true names of these two were (Ivan) Vlado Trichkov and (Gorsho) Delcho Simov.[2] Long and detailed conversations took place. After prolonged bad weather and some failed sorties, supplies eventually rained down into this high Serbian plateau, at Dobro Polje on the night of January 25th. On the same night a second British mission, given the happy code-name of 'Claridges', dropped in. As Mostyn Davies reported:

> Cairo had decided to put in this mission now, rather than wait longer, to assist me in the enormous task of building up a regular Bulgar Partisan force. The idea was that when Mulligatawny moved into Bulgaria, Claridges should remain behind on the frontier and perform the function of a rear base.[3]

For the time being this plan was inoperable. For two months, both missions marched and counter-marched across this snow-covered mountainous terrain, evading police drives and the drives of occupying German and Bulgarian forces. Mulligatawny comprised four men: commanding officer, two wireless operators and an interpreter; Claridges only two, an officer and a wireless operator.

But even this small combined forced constituted an embarrassment to the partisans; requiring horses or mules for their wireless sets, batteries and other equipment, they could

1   WO 204.8709.
2   Inf. from Simov, oral, 1979.
3   The files which contain the messages to and from Bulgaria were in some confusion when the research was done for these lectures. Some had been withdrawn, others were described as being 'in use'. They may be in better order now. The citations throughout these lectures are from the series WO 201/1600, WO 201/1604 and WO 201/1605.

not move fast and quietly by night over trackless terrain, and they were a constant object of enemy pursuit. Each time a dropping pin-point was set up, it required the allocation of two battalions of partisans (normally Serbian) for its defence. Worse, for five whole weeks, subsequent to 4th February, no successful sorties came from Bari: repeatedly sorties were expected, arrangements made; sometimes fires were lighted on the high plateau and nothing came. The explanation usually given was 'met' - the weather. Eventually on 14th March the sorties resumed.

On 18th March the entire South Serbian mountain district was encircled and a major offensive commenced, employing some ten or fifteen thousand troops, the majority Bulgarian army units, with Nedich (Yugoslav collaborationist) auxilliaries. There commenced one of those local epics of the partisan resistance. Partisans and civilian refugees alike were herded upwards on to the freezing inhospitable slopes of Mount Comernik. In repeated desperate battles units broke out in different directions. Every valley and escape-route was invested; partisans and refugees were encircled, broke out, were ambushed, encircled again and again broke out. Most of the surrounding areas were controlled by hostile Chetniks and casualties were appalling. The British mission was split in half, the officers commanding Mulligatawny and Claridges and a W/T operator coming eventually on the 22nd or 23rd of March to an old mill on a mountain stream. Their partisan guard went into the nearby village of Nove Selo to look for food. During the night the mill was attacked, Major Mostyn Davies of Mulligatawny was mortally wounded, his W/T operator was killed, and the officer commanding Claridges mission escaped from a back window of the mill. He hid for a day or two in a hole in the snow, then in a haystack and was fed by a peasant who directed a small partisan unit to his aid. This escort led him to two other survivors of Mulligatawny

18

and together they moved down in the next few days to the Radnovica/Tergoviste area on the margins of South Serbia and Macedonia which was the headquarters of General Apostolski of the Macedonian partisans and of General Vukmanovich (or Tempo), Tito's representative in the region. Here also there was another British mission, code-named Entanglement, equipped with radio. Those of the other missions had been lost in the battle of Mt Comernik. From the rest and comparative luxury of this liberated zone, the officer commanding Claridges found time, on 21st April, to write three letters, one to his parents in England, one to his close friend Iris Murdoch and one to his brother serving in the tanks in Italy. I do not think that I need pretend to disguise any more, for you will know that this brother was myself.

Frank Thompson wrote to his parents 'This letter is rather a long shot since mail in this area isn't very regular. Let's hope it reaches you' and he went on to reassure them 'I've got a remarkably clean pair of heels, and now hold the record for the twenty yards sprint for three major battle areas.'[1]

Captain Frank Thompson - or Major Thompson as he was gazetted at about this time - was twenty-three years old and had been a soldier since September 1939. He had already been serving for three years in the Middle East. He entered the Balkan theatre with experience of active service as well as specialist training, and he had the advantage of a good knowledge of several European languages including Russian, Serbo-Croat and Bulgarian.

From their temporarily secure base in South Serbia, the mission was reorganised. A new W/T was dropped in and a new

1   Letter, Frank Thompson to Edward and Theodosia Thompson, /4/44 (Thompson papers).

19

wireless operator, Sergeant Kenneth Scott. Discussions took place between Generals Apostolski and Tempo, representatives of the Bulgarian partisan movement and the British Mission. The Bulgarian partisan forces were rapidly growing in strength as regular units deserted to the partisans and as volunteers streamed over from the border districts. At the end of April yet another, even greater offensive commenced against the partisans. All units marched north - Macedonian, Kossovan, Serbian, Bulgarian, with the Claridges mission accompanying the headquarters of Apostolski and Tempo.

In spite of the best efforts of expert British anti-historians, known as 'weeders', some of my brother's signals from the field have survived in a wrinkle of the public records covering the period 15th April to 12th May. I will continue the narrative with recourse to these, supplemented by the oral recollections of some of the participants.

On 22nd April Thompson reported that a representative of the Bulgarian partisan G.H.Q. was at Tempo's headquarters planning a joint offensive into Western Bulgaria in the region of Kyustendil. The object was to create some free partisan territory inside Bulgaria and also to draw off some of the Bulgarian occupation forces from Serbia. The plan was to start in a fortnight, and 'OF have promised me I shall be inside Bulgaria in three weeks but have now learnt to treat with reserve all such messages'. There was, as another message made clear 'no free territory anywhere [in Bulgaria] as Yugoslav partisans know it', although in some areas such as Sredna Gora and Trun 'most of the population is pro-partisan.'[1]

---

1   WO201. All the extracts from signals in the following pages are
     from this series unless otherwise noted.

This is perhaps the place at which we should turn briefly aside to enquire who were these Bulgarian partisans? They have been dealt with curtly and ungenerously in most Western historiography, to the point that they vanish altogether from visibility. In Bulgarian historiography, by contrast, they have been rewarded with overflowing measure in an exfoliation of mythology which, to the present day, offers a legitimising heroic ancestry to the ruling regime. We can approach the truth only by way of two provisos, which contrast the Bulgarian with the Yugoslav resistance. First, the Yugoslav resistance assumed the force of a national uprising against foreign occupation, German and Bulgarian. Bulgaria, however, was an Axis ally, although a somewhat odd one. She was at war with the western allies but not, for prudential reasons relating to the pro-Russian, pan-Slavic sentiment of the population, with the Soviet Union. Hence, Bulgaria was not occupied by German troops, although these were present and passed freely through to Greece and to the East, and her own armies were not involved on any major battle front; they remained available for internal policing, and also for occupation duties in those areas - Northern Thrace, Macedonia, Eastern Serbia - which they had, with German permission, annexed. It follows from this that the Bulgarian partisan movement must, perforce, engage not in a national resistance against the occupiers but in a direct insurrectionary action against its own national government, in conditions of almost-impossible difficulty. In each and every action on Bulgarian teritory it must be assumed that every second person might be hostile and a potential informer; the support, refuge, food supplies, recruits, information of entire populations - the water in which the Yugoslav partisan units could so often swim and survive - was denied to the Bulgarian partisans. From the very start of the partisan movement there, from its infinitessimal beginnings in 1942 to the operation of small

21

haiduk bands in 1943, through a period of rapid growth between December 1943 and April/May 1944, and a period of defeat and savage repression, as well as ambiguous leadership, in May-July 1944, it is my firm impression that the major part of all Bulgarian partisan activity was concerned with a desperate effort at mere survival, at being able to eat, to sleep, to stay - for a day or two more - alive. Actions would consist of the rapid descent on a village, an attack on the police station the shooting of a deputy mayor, or the burning of records with possibly the time to make some speeches or gain one or two recruits and above all, to search for food. Only in the final six weeks before the massive insurrection of September 9th and the subsequent entry of the Red Army was the partisan movement of any numerical force and able to pass over to offensive actions. Nineteen-twentieths of those among the ruling group who later claimed partisan credentials were individuals who had entered the movement in those last euphoric weeks.

The second proviso follows from the first. Engaged in desperate marginal actions in a civil war (what many statesmen today would undoubtedly describe as 'terrorism'), the politics of the partisans were subject to continual pressure away from those of national or anti-fascist alliance into more sectarian courses. While a national centre did exist in the Fatherland Front - an alliance of Left Agrarians, Social Democrats and radical army officers (the Zveno group) with the Communists - which issued proclamations in generous anti-fascist rhetoric, in effect the fighting arm of the Fatherland Front was more strictly a Communist organisation than perhaps any other wartime resistance movement. The other participating groups shrank from the adventurism of civil war and supplied few recruits to the partisans. The military command of the partisans was almost wholly Communist, incited onward from time to time by the messages of Georgi

Dimitrov their leader, still in exile in Moscow. Young recruits to the movement, peasants, students, workers, deserting soldiers, might not be Communists, but they came under the instruction of Communist Party political commissars. The objective of the movement, therefore, was that of victory in a civil war, and this coloured partisan tactics. Since there were, until the final weeks, no liberated areas, many potential partisans and their sympathisers remained as sabotage groups in the greater security of the towns, preparing for the insurrection of September 9th.

When we have made these two provisos, though, it is not necessary to go on to be curt and ungenerous. The Bulgarian partisan movement functioned in extraordinarily disadvantageous conditions which, perforce, accentuated its narrow sectarian character. But for those very reasons the courage demanded of the Bulgarian partisan was perhaps even greater than that of his Yugoslav opposite number.The regular Bulgarian occupation forces in Serbia and Thrace were noted for their brutality in the face of hostile civilian populations. Most murders were accompanied by torture, most rapes were aggravated and ended with murder. In Serbia the village of Bojnik is remembered as the Czechs remember Lidice. Here, on 17th February 1942, the entire village population was assembled and massacred for the offence of having sheltered partisans. Four hundred and seventy-six inhabitants were killed on that day; the gravestones show whole families from elders in their seventies to three-month-old infants buried together. Those Bulgarian soldiers who, disgusted by their fellows and imbued with a perhaps exalted and simplistic pro-Soviet and anti-fascist idealism, deserted and threw in their lot with the partisans could expect - should they fall into the hands of the partisan-hunters, who were indeed head-hunters, not death only, but the most protracted and foul death that ingenuity could devise. For the women among them

23

every form of sexual assault and humiliation would precede their execution. These were people of courage and, in the main, not ideologues at all but simple people from hard and poor backgrounds with family traditions of resistance to police and army often going back to 1923 and the two abortive insurrections, one Agrarian and one Communist, which followed upon the assassination of the Agrarian leader Stambouliski, and to the years of repression which followed them. I need not tell you that Bulgaria in the 1930s and early '40s was not a pleasant Western democracy. One way of dealing with offenders, after the rising of 1923, had been to throw them alive into the furnaces of Sofia's central police station. By 1943 it was, perhaps, a place somewhat like El Salvador.

The remarkable thing about the Bulgarian partisan movement is not the fact that its presence was smaller than those of Yugoslavia,Greece and Albania, but that it existed at all. Despite the determined attempts of a small handful, no serious armed resistance developed in two neighbouring Axis nations, Roumania and Hungary. Bulgarians have reason to be proud of their partisans, although they do not, for that reason, have the right to falsify the evidence and to mythologise its savage fugitive reality.

Let us return to our narrative. There is 'no free territory anywhere in Bulgaria as the Yugoslav partisans know it' Frank Thompson signalled to his HQ, SOE Cairo, at the end of April. On 23rd April the Trun odred (partisan unit) came in to the HQ to await re-equipment with British arms and reformation as the First Partisan Brigade. Its leader, Slavcho Trunski came, like other notable partisan leaders, including Znepolski and Balkansky, from only two or three miles across the old Serbian frontier. This whole mountainous district, from Trun in Bulgaria to Crna Trava in Serbia, had certain common features, ethnically, occupationally and in way of life. A high proportion of the male workers were seasonal building workers, absent from their mountain farms for some months every year, when the women folk assumed the farming and household roles on their own. In return, the men brought their building skills back to the mountains and the area, served only by mule-tracks and in winter bullock-drawn sledges, boasted comfortable and substantially-built houses.

Trunski himself, who was to be, thirty-five years later General Trunski, Deputy Minister of Defence and our host in that black official car, had been a building worker as a boy, then an agronomy student and a part-time actor in a travelling theatre. He was one of the first, most heroic and most successful of the partisans. Having the partially liberated territory of South Serbia at their backs, the Trun odred made repeated forays into Bulgarian territory. The fraternal interoperation of these two national movements, in despite of the sombre and bloody background of Bulgarian/Serbian fratricide, was itself a remarkable and hopeful historical event, perhaps made possible only by the mutual adoption of an internationalist Communist ideology. On 24th April, Major Thompson signalled that the last bone of contention between them had been discreetly buried:

> OF have changed attitude Macedonian question to come into line with Jugoslav movement. Free independent Macedonia now branded as Mihailovist slogan and new war cry is 'National Self-Determination on basis of Atlantic Charter.' Now it appears to be up to the Macedonians.

The tone of the signal appears sceptical. The bone has been given only a shallow burial.

On 25th April Thompson signalled that the partisan leader 'Ivan' or 'Georgi', who was at their HQ, had revealed himself to be the C-in-C of the Bulgarian partisan movement. 'Ivan fought as junior officer Salonika campaign and is aged

46. Has very good brain and broad European outlook but as yet have no opportunity to assess his military powers.' Ivan's true name was Vlado Trichkov, a metal-worker and trade unionist who owed his position not only to his age and military experience but also to his status within the Communist Party.

On the next day the First and Second Sofia brigades were formally founded from the nuclei of the Trun and Botevgrad odreds respectively, together with fresh contingents of army deserters and new recruits. The brigades had, as uniforms, only caps which 'look very smart and soldierly.' In every message now, Thompson called urgently for arms as well as for other items - boots, binoculars, compasses, watches, more W/T sets. 'Everything depends on getting larger arms supply to quicken whole partisan movement.'

At the same time he pleaded with his HQ to delay a little longer before sending in a further British mission under the command of Major Anthony Strachey. No odred in Bulgaria could afford the 'luxury' of a mission and its equipment - rapid and constant movement was their only security. What was required immediately was 'maximum sorties soonest. One plane now will be worth five in three weeks time.' He advised also against the dropping, blind, into the Rhodope mountains of a further British mission commanded by Major Temple:

> Georgi [Trichkov] says Partisans have semi-free territory there. Partisans use this term to denote area where they have to run like hell whole time but have local population fairly friendly. My guess is that… Temple will spend first fortnight in Bulgary running hard and will be lucky if he keeps communication. Here, however, we have free territory behind us and safe support of Tempo and Yugoslav Partisans.

On 29th April Thompson addressed directly to Captain Hugh Seton Watson, who was in charge of the Bulgarian desk at SOE Cairo, a request for 'general directive soonest':

Realise I have not got full picture but suggest any plan should be based on following assumptions

1) that 20 years of Fascism have demoralised Bulgarians to such an extent that NO repeat NO large scale revolt by Army and People against Germans can be expected. General collapse on Italian lines is most to be hoped for, with harassing action by active OF supporters. Working class revolt in Sofia, Plovdiv and Varna possibly.

2) That Bulgarian partisan movement although it has wide popular support is too badly armed and scattered to be made into serious nation wide force before big day.

On these two assumptions he advised firstly the continued bombing of military targets, secondly the building up of strong forces capable of harassing the westerly and southerly communications of Sofia and thirdly, as a lower priority 'if there is still time when this has been done', the reinforcing with arms of partisan units active in the Plovdiv and Botevgrad districts.

There are two points to be made about this rather sober message. First, it does not confirm subsequent suggestions that Thompson's notions of possibility at this time were euphoric and romantic: that he saw himself as a 'Lawrence of Bulgaria' riding on a mule at the head of a ragged detachment into the cheering crowds of liberated Bulgaria.[1] Second, I can find no evidence anywhere that this urgent call for a reply and a 'general directive soonest' was ever answered. The evidence

1   For example, Stowers Johnson, *Agents Extraordinary*, (London, Robert Hale, 1975) The title alone is misleading here, since these men were not 'agents' but British Liaison Officers, not involved with intelligence.

may of course have been destroyed by one of the brilliant weeders or anti-historians to whom I have referred. But Professor Seton Watson cannot himself recall sending any reply. If the message lingered unanswered on his Cairo desk, this should not be imputed to his inattention. Other arguments were going on at the very highest level of allied command - arguments to which I shall return later - which must have made it exceptionally difficult for a low-ranking officer in Cairo to send to his officer in the field any directive at all. It was a remarkably improvisatory and amateurish set-up. On the one hand SOE Cairo was sending missions into the field, and into desperately exposed fields at that, and was pressing to send even more; on the other hand there was no authoritative directive to these missions as to what they should do nor were they being offered adequate arms and support.

The Bulgarian mission as well had precious little in the way of supplies. There had been a hiatus in supples to Major Mostyn Davies between 4th February and 14th March. The reason given was always 'met' and sometimes at least this clearly was the reason. Another plane got through on 17th March and three others failed owing to 'met'. No drops could of course be made or received during the battle of Mt Comernik and its aftermath. Some supplies came in on 7th April when Sergeant Scott and his WT were sent in, but I can find no evidence of further drops in the rest of April. On 26th April, Thompson's message was distinctly sharp. Planes had made successful sorties that night to a nearby mission with the Yugoslav partisans:

> This had disastrous effect on waiting Bulgars who had been told only bad weather held up help for them. Essential position clarified at once. Comment most urgently and tell me your plans. What do I tell them now?

After this the mission and the combined HQs were being

driven north by the enemy offensive. War Office signals show that now, at last, Claridges had been placed on priority for sorties. But with the mission continually in movement, and with military conditions permitting the preparation and holding of any pinpoint for only two or three days at the most, sorties were impossible. The signal received on 3rd May reads: 'We are being chased by Bulgars... Pinpoint closed. Cheerio'.

Matters were further confused by a characteristic military balls-up. Command of the operation was located in Cairo, but SOE was half-way through the process of moving its HQ to southern Italy at Bari. Major James Klugman was the officer in charge of the Bari sub-desk,[1] and it was from a Bari airfield that the sorties were actually flown. The balls-up was this; when Sergeant Scott had been dropped in to join Claridges, his Cairo code-book had been dropped to a different mission altogther, somewhere in Thrace. Without a code all messages would be open to interception and therefore could not be sent. Thompson was trying to sort this out, suggesting for the cipher the novel *Death before Honour* 'of which we have a copy, first 99 pages, first five words of two successive lines'. Maybe Cairo did not have a copy of *Death before Honour*. In any case signals continued to be transmitted through the only available route, on the code of the Entanglement mission, which code, however, for reasons which I do not understand, was only decipherable at Bari. So the position was that every Claridges signal had first to go to

---

1   James Klugman [190? - 1981] had been a leading figure in the international Communist student movement before the war. Some proponents of conspiracy theories have suggested a sinister role for him in his post at Bari.

Bari, which was desperately understaffed with cipher clerks, be thence recorded and transmitted to Cairo, where it was decoded once more and a reply encoded and sent to Bari. Here it was decoded, transcribed into Entanglement code and sent to Claridges. Meanwhile, of course, pin points had been lost under the pressure of the enemy advance. On 3rd May Cairo received an urgent message:

> Personal from Klugman. Feel strongly essential sorties for Claridges should be laid on in Bari until Claridges has direct link with Cairo. Unless this done serious errors are inevitable as all Serbian pinpoints unstable.

I am sure that there will be those who will find in this evidence of atrocious Communist conspiracy. But if one holds the emergencies of the time in mind, it seems to me to be only good sense.

On 5th May Thompson and Dugmore, the officer in charge of Entanglement, sent out a joint signal:

> At Crna Trava with Tempo, Georgi, Apostolski...and Bulgarian HQ. One brigade and 1000 unarmed men. All of us driven here by big Bulgarian offensive. Imperative have arms and food soonest for this joint force...

The signal is annotated - perhaps by Klugman? - 'Have signalled Thompson sorties standing by. Can he receive Strachey?' Thompson signalled 'Offensive grows in weight and we march again tonight.' Apostolski was advising that it was unsafe to send sorties for three days 'want Strachey as soon as things calm down.' The partisans and three hundred unarmed Bulgarian volunteers were starving; food must be dropped with the arms.

The climax of the retreat was reached on the four days of 9th to 12th May. The combined partisan forces temporarily stabilised their position and held a good dropping ground -

probably at Dobro Polje, or possibly nearer to Kalna a village close to the Bulgarian frontier. On 9th May the First Sofia Brigade, formed from a few members of the old Trun odred and 300 new recruits, commenced to move into Bulgaria with arms borrowed from Serbian partisans, under the command of Slavcho Trunski. The Second Sofia Brigade, comprising the rest of the old Trun odred with recruits, some 200 strong, commanded by Dencho Znepolski, was cut off and engaged in extremely heavy fighting in the Osogovska hills, but expected to break through shortly. In response to the repeated pressure from Cairo to push in Strachey or other new British missions, Thompson signalled that the partisans: 'state quite impossible to take BLO at present but in fortnights time if we have had large number sorties position may be altered'. A further message was sharper:

> very reasonably Apostolski refuses to accept responsibility for any more missions until present offensive has turned corner. We have eight Englishmen here now which is thought maximum handicap for any partisan unit entered for Spring gallop.

Cairo, which had failed to reply to his eleven-day-old request for a 'directive', now offered not only Major Strachey but also an Engineering Officer. 'Who is Engineer Officer?' Thompson snapped 'and what is he going to engineer in these mountains? See NO repeat NO point in dropping valuable Sappers to Bulgarian mission until they are set up in Bulgaria.' It was clear that still, on 9th May, Thompson had no settled plan to enter Bulgaria. By now the Second Sofia Brigade had broken through to Kalna, exhausted and depleted but 'in terrific heart' after five days of heavy fighting. They began reforming to strike into Bulgaria. Thompson proposed to remain in the frontier district with another British mission, commanded by Major Saunders, attached to the Serbian partisans, and to run a joint dropping ground to serve both movements.

On the nights of the 10th and 11th, at long last, the sky thundered and the air was full of containers; perhaps as many as thirty successful sorties were made, half to the Bulgars half to the Serbs. Thompson signalled the delegates' warmest thanks 'This is the biggest encouragement Bulgarians have had since Mostyn arrived…after last night and a few more like it stream [of recruits] may well become torrent.'

But the mission was now again on the run. A shortage of horses had meant that the charging engine for the batteries had been left behind. A new code-pad had arrived and in future all signals were to go to Cairo. The message containing these instructions ends with a desperate signal from Captain Sale, the officer in charge of organising sorties from Bari:

> As result of unusually high pressure work last three days Bari secretarial staff cannot accept my work. Unless secretary for self arrives soon messages will be seriously delayed. No transport. No clerk. No office equipment. No secretary. No hope.

This is where the evidence of Thompson's signals ends. Major Saunders signalled 'Left HQ hastily on 12th…chased by Bulgarians. Running since… Thompson left earlier 12th. Met Thompson during gallop. He going Bulgaria.' In a subsequent message Saunders reported that before leaving for Bulgaria Claridges W/T had only two bad batteries and a hand charger, and all equipment had fallen in the river during the march. That is the reason why no further messages were received from Claridges until some four weeks later when the set, now in enemy hands, had been repaired by German technicians. So the factual answer to our eminent host, in the black Volga car, was simply that Cairo could not possibly have informed the Bulgarian authorities as to the Second Sofia Brigade's progress since the W/T was inoperable, Cairo had received no signals and knew nothing. No message at all was received from Claridges after 11th May.

The factual answer to the drunken gossip of British Intelligence to the effect that Frank Thompson crossed into Bulgaria contrary to orders and forcing his sergeant at gun point and that he was subsequently betrayed by the partisans for gold is that this too is a lie. Sergeant Scott who survived the march but has been prevented from publishing his own account by a marvellous British anti-historical device known as the Official Secrets Act, has told me that it is a lie. He decoded every message received from Cairo via Bari, and no such order was received. He was scandalised by the suggestion that he had been forced by threats to take part, and regarded it as an imputation upon his honour. Moreover I have read the full record of his debriefing in 1945 and nothing of this sort appears in it.

That part of the tale then is a lie. So far as crossing into Bulgaria is concerned, there is nothing very remarkable in that decision. Mostyn Davies had been operating for weeks on the frontier, in territory annexed to Bulgaria and occupied by Bulgarian forces. From the point of view of the Bulgarian authorities they had been in Bulgaria for some time already. Mulligatawny's original brief had been to move into Bulgaria, while Claridges was to safeguard supplies on the frontier; when Mostyn Davies was killed the missions and briefs of Mulligatawny and Claridges had been merged, at least until Strachey or another mission could come in. In more than one of his signals Thompson had mentioned his expectations of moving into Bulgaria and there is no evidence that Cairo did anything to check his intentions. Finally there is an obvious if humdrum point. Where else, on 12th May, could Claridges go? The partisans were encircled by greatly superior forces and the net was drawing uncomfortably tight. The partisan strategy was to strike out simultaneously in several directions - the

Serbs north-west, the Macedonians south, the Kossovans south-west, the First Sofia Brigade south-east and the Second Sofia Brigade north-east. To remain within the net when the other partisans had all broken out would have been perilous in the extreme, and moreover the mission was attached to no other formation, but to the Bulgarian partisans. On 25th April in the nearest thing to a directive in the record, Cairo signalled: 'Thompson should remain longest possible with OF delegates and failing this with Trun odred' and a summary of the events said 'Claridges has been instructed by Cairo to remain with Bulgarian general staff...and was therefore obliged to move with them'.

These are plain and good enough reasons. Some six weeks later, after the mission had met with disaster, the Bulgarian Section was prevaricating on the matter... 'Thompson decision to go was forced on him by attitude Bulgarian delegates and not repeat not ordered by us.' This is true only in the sense that Cairo gave no order of any kind to Thompson. He was left to his own discretion in the field and his urgent request for briefing went unanswered. The reason why Cairo found it necessary to prevaricate in June 1944 may become clearer later.

It may also become clearer then that the matter was a good deal more complex than I have so far suggested. For the Second Sofia Brigade was not just breaking out of encirclement and making a foray into Bulgarian territory or a feint to draw off enemy forces. It was embarking on a much more ambitious plan - no less than a march, accompanied by the General Staff and the British Mission, which was planned to pass north of Sofia and penetrate into the Sredna Gora range in south central Bulgaria and there to proclaim a free partisan territory, north of Plovdiv, and establish a new centre of command.

The march ended in disaster. The aim appears to have

been to transfer to central Bulgaria an efficient fighting group together with the British liaison mission in order to organise resistance in the areas nearer the cities and to secure reinforcement in the form of air-dropped supplies from the British. The Second Sofia Brigade were to accompany the British mission and march swiftly north of Sofia to join up with the partisans thought to be operating in the Stara Planina mountains and go with them down to the Sredna Gora. Here they hoped to establish an area of liberated territory and to receive arms and supplies from the air-drops.

When the various partisan groups broke out in different directions, the Second Sofia Brigade moved quietly north, evading the military and police posts. The military seem to have turned their main forces at this stage towards Trunski and the First Brigade who were moving east. The Second Brigade meanwhile continued northwards, crossing the Sofia-Belgrade railway and swinging north-east to the Bulgarian border. They pushed on steadily, taking only short breaks of three or four hours for sleep, and eventually dropped down from the wooded hills of the border country to the remote village of Dolgi Del. Here they apparently abandoned all attempt at secrecy, entering the village in daylight, seizing the police officer and tax collector, giving them a brief 'trial' before shooting them and burning the tax and police records.

At Dolgi Del Scott was able to get his W/T batteries recharged at a primitive water-powered generating plant. After a brief stay they left the scene of their triumph, in the early morning and set off eastwards, avoiding most of the anti-partisan posts which were established throughout the district, but jettisoning light equipment, including their typewriters, to gain greater speed. It was raining continuously, and on the higher ground there was dense mountain mist. Their equipment was minimal,they had no maps apart from the parachute-silk map of the Balkans which was part of Frank

35

Thompson's basic equipment, and clearly they lost their directions in the mountain mist. As they approached their destination there were arguments among them as to the best method of proceeding. The advice of Balkansky prevailed, and the group abandoned any attempt at secrecy and went ahead, holding meetings in the villages, burning documents and recruiting members for their group. On 21st May they reached the river Iskar. Their whole tactic rested on the hope of meeting a major partisan group, the Chavdar partisans, who would have arms and supplies, including food. But the Chavdar partisans had been wiped out by a government offensive before they arrived, and when they came to the district they found only burnt-out houses and a hostile population. Finally, hungry and exhausted, they fell asleep in scrub woodland on a hillside near the village of Batoulia. The guides whom they had conscripted in the village left them while they slept and betrayed their position to the authorities. In the battle that ensued the group was split up. Thompson and his sergeant escaped with the largest group, but within a few days they were again surrounded and eventually those who were not killed, including Scott and Thompson, were taken prisoner. I will come back to this story.

We are now in a position to return to the technical questions of method, myth and anecdote which are the main theme of this lecture. The close-up narrative which I have offered may appear at first glance to be straightforward enough. Here is a sequence of episodes each of which appears to lead directly into the next, under the pressure of pursuits and emergencies.

Yet, at a far remove behind this we can sense the distant pressure of other issues. What was the interest of the Western alliance in Bulgaria as a theatre of operations? What was the interest of SOE Cairo? Were there competing interests within SOE itself - as for example those of James Klugman at Bari?

What was the character of the Bulgarian partisan movement, its objectives and strategies? How and by whom were these determined? Were serious tactical or political blunders committed in the pursuit of these objectives?

Even in 1947 when I made my first visit to Bulgaria, these questions were highly loaded. They remained and remain sensitive. Certain questions clearly provoked discomfort many years after the events, and these sensitivities increased rather than diminished over the years. As the Cold War developed it required on both sides a continual reprocessing of approved views of the past (or amnesia about the past) and the accretion of new dimensions of myth. Let us look briefly at some of these points, first in Bulgaria and then in Britain. In no East European country did the brief moment of anti-fascist alliance collapse more rapidly than in Bulgaria. The insurrection of September 9th 1944 was followed by immediate limitation of western influence in the country; old scores were paid off, executions took place in the towns and in the country. The agrarian leader Nikola Petkov was tried and convicted and then, after the Cominform expulsion of Yugoslavia the Bulgarian Communist Party was purged and a trial staged of its secretary Traicho Kostov.

I am not an authority on Bulgarian politics and I cannot even read their language. But I can discern four distinct stages of retrospective myth. In the first, from 1945 to about 1948 Major Frank Thompson was a National Hero of Bulgaria, Byronic in stature. A railway station north of Sofia was renamed Major Thompson station. Modest memorials were raised in his memory. In 1947 when my mother and I visited Bulgaria we were received with genuine popular enthusiasm as state visitors, entertained by Georgi Dimitrov, received formally in the National Theatre and conducted along the route of the march and the battle by partisan survivors. A second phase began after the Kostov trial when an internal power-struggle took place in the Bulgarian Communist party between the Moscow-trained and the home-grown leaders. Some of the former partisans, including Trunsky and Znepolski, were disgraced and imprisoned. It was discovered that the party had been infiltrated by Western imperialist agents. So successful had this penetration been in Yugoslavia - for example the Conservative Member of Parliament and Scottish laird Sir Fitzroy Maclean and Churchill's own son at Tito's headquarters - that the entire regime had been detached from the socialist camp. Western agents had had less success in Bulgaria, but all the former partisan leaders in Western Bulgaria were under suspicion as possible Titoist collaborators.

This reading of history might have entailed the total historical disgrace of Major Thompson. But here there was wrinkle within a wrinkle. No less an authority than Harry Pollitt, General secretary of the Communist Party of Great Britain had formally announced at the Bulgarian Communist Party congress of 1948 that Major Thomspon had been a member of the CPGB. He was (it could now be revealed) a well-intentioned young man of courage and commitment to the partisan cause who had been used by the imperialists. In this internal communist party historiography, Major Mostyn Davies appeared as the imperialist villain. The treatment of Thompson remained ambiguous. Whether he was actually demoted from the status of National Hero I do not know - I think it probably became a profoundly silent area, although I have been told of derogatory references to him as a member of a wealthy landowning family with property in Greece. A third change occurred during the Khrushchev era. New power-struggles within the party led to the disgrace of Chervenkov, Chankov and co, and the release and rehabilitation of most of the old partisans. In the late '50s and early '60s the presses were flooded with partisan reminiscences. In the 1970s immense and ostentatious memorials were erected at the site of partisan actions. The cult of the partisan coincided with the rise of Todor Zhivkov as leader of the Communist Party and partisan ancestry became part of a necessary legitimating mythology.

Partly as a consequence of this thaw, and of the partial rehabilitation of some of his old associates, Major Thompson emerged again into the history in the late '70s. His name was added to the partisan memorials and a day nursery was named after him in Sofia. My wife and I, attempting to visit the country as private tourists in 1979 were hijacked as official visitors of the state and entertained, now with warm hospitality, now with official courtesy, now with unctious officious propaganda for which our officially-appointed interpreter apologised once we were out of earshot. A film and a book about Major Thompson, the latter in English and entitled Grateful Bulgaria were produced, perhaps as much for the burgeoning tourist trade as for the historical record. The rehabilitation of the British mission remained qualified. The NCOs who had lost their lives were grudgingly admitted, but Major Mostyn Davies remained unrecognised, suspected of being an imperialist agent. The archives, when we were in the country, remained closed, and publications of the period 1945-48 remained rare and inaccessible. There was no sense in 1979 that the actions and decisions of the partisan era could be researched into and discussed with any idea of historical objectivity. One sensed that there was a deliberate ambiguity of interpretation, that documents and anecdotes were being held in reserve, just below the counter, which might be pulled out and used for whatever political cause was in the running; perhaps, we thought in 1979, the partisan experience might provide ammunition of some sort for the running word-battle then proceding about the Macedonian question.

It is clear from all this that a good deal of so-called 'oral history' reminiscence is structured as myth, unless it is collected at completely unrehearsed meetings of observers. We found, for example, many accounts of these same events on the Serbian side of the frontier in the high districts of Crna Trava, Dobro Polje and Kalna which seemed to contain far less structuring and retrospective selective interference, apart perhaps from a certain colouring of heroic myth. In Bulgaria, however, even the most readily-available anecdotes seemed no more than a code for ideology. This coding may be well-intentioned, as was the story we were told of Major Thompson's exit from the ambush in the mill after the death of Mostyn Davies with a blazing revolver in either hand. Here the account picks up something from the heroic myth of the Western and may intend no harm. But it too has aspects of coded ideology, distinguishing between the good Englishman, Thompson the communist and the bad, Davies the imperialist agent.

Mostyn Davies had been given, in all the Bulgarian accounts, treatment that was mean and unworthy. He was accused of being a spy and of deliberately preventing the sending of sorties with supplies and arms. His personality did not lend itself easily to heroic treatment, and the fact that he did not speak any of the Balkan languages meant that he did not make the same contacts and friendships that Thompson was able to make. He suffered dreadfully from the cold in that long winter in the mountains and reminiscences repeatedly made fun of his misery, of the icicles on his nose, his clinging to the warmth of the stove and his indignation at the repeated forced marches at night to evade pursuit. Yet it was Davies who first established a mission with the Bulgarians; it was his reports back to Cairo which committed British policy to their support and which brought in the Claridges mission. He lost his life in the work just as certainly as did Thompson, and if the British missions did serve the Bulgarian cause in those months, it was owing first of all to Davies.[1]

I hope that this explanation is now clear. When General Trunski turned to us on that day in 1979 in the Volga car and announced 'It is said that the Second Sofia Brigade was defeated because the British Liaison staff were reporting daily to Cairo, and Cairo was then sending messages to the Bulgarian army as to the route of the march and the location of the partisans', his statement had nothing to do with historical evidence at all. It was simply ideological attribution, coded as anecdote. The ideology preceded the history, and invented an anecdote to conform to it. The demands of the ideological script were these - the heroic Second Sofia Brigade could not possibly have met with disastrous defeat through any blunders or inadequacy of its own, it must have, somehow, been 'betrayed'. Clearly the betrayers must have been imperialist agents - but, wait a minute - the particular British agent accompanying the march is still (for certain purposes) a National Hero of Bulgaria. Harry Pollitt had announced at a CP conference that he was a communist and that is irrefutable evidence. Also, when captured, Major Thompson revealed nothing to his captors in spite of brutal interrogation and when he was subsequently executed conducted himself with personal heroism. Here are contradictory signals which cannot easily be encoded in a single anecdote. But ah, a resolution

1   Note by D.T. On a visit to Bulgaria in 1994 (see Epilogue) I was told by Bulgarians that the British Liaison officers had been represented to them first as heroic allies in the fight against fascism, then as imperialist agents infiltrating on behalf of the Western Allies, then - after 1991 - as Soviet agents intent on establishing Soviet hegemony.

suggests itself. If Major Thompson cannot himself have betrayed the partisans directly to the Bulgarian authorities, no doubt his signals could have been treacherously relayed onwards from Cairo. Thompson remains a hero, both he and the partisans are betrayed by imperialist double-dealing. We have a perfect ideological fit.

In fact, of course, no 'explanation' of the defeat is required at all. The explanation, if any, must be as to how the partisans ever allowed themselves to get into that utterly exposed position. No signals interception was needed for the Bulgarian authorities to plot their movements. Some two hundred partisans were threading their way through a countryside thick with informers and police posts; sometimes they moved openly by day, even entering villages for meetings; they had no guides; they had no food; they were only an hour or so by motorised transport away from Sofia; in the immediate district through which they were passing were some twelve thousand troops and armed police. It was a military folly of the first order, justifiable only in terms of a symbolic confrontation, terms perhaps similar to those of the Dublin Easter rising of 1916. We need no fabricated anecdote of 'betrayal'.

Bowed with years I stand before you and offer you my methodological advice, the fruit of many years of research. It is this. If you find yourself in the back of an official Volga car, talking through an interpreter to a high military officer of a Warsaw Pact country, then watch it. Even when talking to more humble and disinterested persons, remember that the memory is the most imperfect and selective vector of evidence. 'Facts' can still be codes or myths, one must already know a great deal to be able to sift evidence from romance; and what one may, most helpfully, gain from oral evidence is most often the marginal, the contingent, the 'colour' of an event. Historians must still depend most heavily on written

42

evidence, not because it has any special truth, but because it is most likely to be contemporaneous with the event.

*****

All that I have written so far refers only to the Communist world, whose mendacity is well-known. Here, in the free world, we can of course pursue quietly our scholarly researches, immune from any ideological intrusion, in complete integrity. If the Bulgarian retrospective reprocessing of this moment in history had, by the end of the '70s, gone through at least four stages, I am happy to say that the official British position had been throughout one of inflexible unwavering uniformity. From 1945 to 1981 it never changed. Not a single official eyelid batted. The position was one of monolithic silence. British aid to Bulgarian partisans was defined, by silence, as a non-event, an unhappening.

No official statement acknowledging this aid has ever been made. The papers of SOE remain closed to research, and such papers of the Foreign and War Offices as have been released have been carefully weeded by anti-historians. I will speculate on some of the probable reasons for this in my final lecture.

In spite of this official silence, however, and in conjunction with it, it has been possible for certain impressions from 'people who know' to get about. It is a very British process by which certain persons (who might be described as unofficial Establishment 'leakers') are a good deal less inhibited by the Official Secrets Act than others, and by which the old ruling-class tradition of gossip in clubs, bars and common rooms provides a certain approved memory of things.

This impression has emphasised two matters. First, Frank Thompson was a Communist. Second, he ventured into Bulgaria not upon orders but upon his private initiative. Now in a curious way this enables anecdotes to circulate as ideological code for a mirror-image of the official Bulgarian story. This code is also a retrospective construct, deriving from the premises not of 1943-44 but of the Cold War. It enables the British authorities to excuse themselves of any responsibility, even of any involvement, in the event. It also enables them to deny any reality to Bulgarian partisans' resistance, or to disparage them as bandits. Frank Thompson may be allowed, in more sympathetic accounts, to be a naive romantic idealist, a self-appointed 'Lawrence of Bulgaria', the sole author of his own fate. Everyone thereby, except Thompson and those bandits, is let off the hook. In less sympathetic and more ideologically-noxious cold-war accounts, Thompson assumes his place in a conspiracy of Communist moles within SOE, master-minded by the notorious James Klugman.

That, decoded, is the ideology which formed the half-drunken anecdote of the former British intelligence officer. Thompson defied orders in entering Bulgaria, he threatened his W/T sergeant and was then betrayed for his gold. The anecdote has a perfect ideological fit, but is as big a lie as the Bulgarian one, and much meaner.

Lecture Two

I COME from a family of compulsive hoarders of paper. As I grow older I am filled with increasing alarm. Am I really going to pass on that load of bric-a-brac, mementos, nostalgias, account books, diaries, to be an anxiety to my children? From the side of my mother, the daughter of American missionaries in the Lebanon, come the papers of early missionaries, of great grandfather Jessup and his family and of their life in that country and in the United States[1]; from my father's side, accounts of his own educational missionary work in Bengal before World War I, and then, after his break with the Methodist church, his voluminous manuscripts, poetry, histories, novels, as well as his correspondence with Indian writers and national leaders including Tagore, Gandhi and Nehru.[2] Then there are boxes and boxes of my own papers. Some of these help to illuminate the vigorous opposition within the British Communist Party and the angry

---

1   The main part of the Jessup papers have now been deposited in the Yale Divinity Library.
2   The papers of E.J. Thompson have been deposited at the Bodleian Library Oxford where they have been catalogued and are now available to scholars.

breach in 1956, the formation of the first New Left and its journals as well as a certain amount of history - the raw material for half-finished books on William Blake and on *Customs in Common*.[1] My wife and I (for she has her load of papers also) wade through the boxes, cartons and files, the false starts and the unfinished lives of yesteryear. One day - and it is coming soon - we shall simply disappear under our own funeral pyre of manuscript detritus, then all that will be needed will be a torch set to our house.

Frank Thompson, my only sibling, was a hoarder also, and his papers fill a case or two. These comprise his letters to his family, his poems and stories and a package of his 'effects', returned from Cairo after he had been posted 'Missing, believed killed' in Bulgaria. These effects are a remarkable collection; they include letters received by him from family and friends during his war service in the Middle and Near East, and several priceless diaries of service in the Western Desert and in the Sicilian landings and of his training as a parachutist. Together they make up a remarkable, if partial, documentation of a life closed before he reached the age of twenty-four.

Frank Thompson was born in August 1920 in India and was named after a paternal uncle, an ardent member of the Independent Labour Party who had been killed in France in the last weeks of the First World War. His father was a writer who taught, part-time, Bengali and Indian history at Oxford

---

1   The papers of E.P. and Dorothy Thompson are being sorted and will eventually with those of Frank Thompson end up in the Bodleian. Some of the papers relating to the years 1956-60 which pair up with ours have been deposited by John Saville in the University of Hull library.

University. Frank attended a robust, elite preparatory school in Oxford, noted for its scholarship rating in the Classical languages, won a scholarship to Winchester College and entered Oxford University, again on a scholarship, in the autumn of 1938. In September 1939, one year later, war broke out and he volunteered for the Royal Artillery. He was then just nineteen. Eighteen months later, in March 1941, he left for the Middle East as a lieutenant in a small communications and intelligence outfit known as GHQ Liaison Regiment (or Phantom) to serve in the Western Desert, Egypt, Iran, Iraq, Jordan, Syria and the Lebanon, Palestine, Sicily and, at last, in Serbia and Bulgaria. Thus, for over three years at an age when today's analogues might be dropping in and out of universities, he was leading an itinerant military life. From the age of twenty, sharp episodes of engagement alternated with longer periods of inactivity and ennui, interspersed with occasional spells of leave in Cairo, Alexandria and the Lebanon until the end of his life shortly before the age of twenty-four.

These last years concern me most since there is something in that aberrant, sometimes exotic, fugitive military culture which, to my knowledge, has been little recorded and which perhaps subsequent generations have passed over with the stereotypes of *Catch 22*. But before I go further I should explain a little more my own relationship with the subject of this lecture.

That Frank Thompson was my brother tells us something; we shared the same parents and the same Oxford home which was supportive, liberal, anti-imperialist, quick with ideas and poetry and international visitors. Of all this I will say very little, in part because the habitus of childhood is so much assumed that one cannot record it objectively, in part because some personal recollections cannot be exposed in public lectures. What I must go on to say is that fraternal relationship does not ensure an identity of experience. Every one with siblings knows this of themselves, yet they often forget it when regarding others. I was three and a half years younger than Frank - not a large gap in time, but a gap that was enlarged by the pressure of the times. When war broke out, Frank was nineteen, I was fifteen. Frank's adult consciousness commenced to mature in the thirties; boyhood friends fought and died with the International Brigade in Spain. In 1937, when he was seventeen, Frank wrote two poems with the title 'To a Communist Friend': the first was dated July:

> Here, in the tranquil fragrance of the honeysuckle
> The gentle, soothing velvet of the foxgloves,
> The cuckoo's drowsy laugh, - I thought of you,
> The ever-whirring dynamos of your will,
> Body and brain, one swift harmonious strength,
> Flashing like polished steel to rid the world
> Of all its gross unfairness. - But the grossest
> Unfairness of it all is that tomorrow,
> When both of us are gone, my sloth, your energy,
> The world will still be cruelly perverse.
> - Why not enjoy the foxgloves while they last?

The second was dated December:

> A year ago in the drowsy Vicarage garden,
> We talked of politics; you, with your tawny hair
> Flamboyant, flaunting your red tie, unburdened
> Your burning heart of the dirge we always hear -
> The rich triumphant and the poor oppress'd.
> And I laughed, seeing, I thought, an example of vague
> ideals not tried but taken on trust,
> That would not stand the test. It sounded all too simple.
>
> A year has passed; and now, where harsh winds rend
> The street's last shred of comfort - past the dread
> Of bomb or gunfire, rigid on the ground

48

Of some cold stinking alley near Madrid,
Your mangled body festers - an example
Of something tougher. - Yet it still sounds all too simple.

Between the two poems his friend Anthony Carritt had been killed fighting with the International Brigade. By the time he went to Oxford Frank had become very aware of the crisis of European politics.

By contrast, my own adult consciousness began to mature in the years of war; I was a product of the forties. And then, from the time that war broke out, we saw each other very little; I was at boarding school, he was in the army. We met on occasional leaves until the time when in March 1941 he was posted overseas. He was then twenty, I had just passed my seventeenth birthday. I did not see him again and we continued to reach each other only through letters.

He has been, from that time, always ahead of me, always three and a half years older, fixed for ever in seniority even to this day, although I have now passed, by over thirty years, his age at death. Yet this has been, like most relationships, a contradictory one. On one hand I respected him as one can only respect an older sibling of genius. From my childhood I had known that he was a scholar and linguist of extraordinary gifts - composing fluent Greek and Latin verse at the age of ten or eleven and, by the age of twenty-three, having command of Latin, ancient and modern Greek, French, German, Italian, Russian, Polish, Serbo-Croat and Bulgarian, as well as a smattering of Arabic. In a characteristic letter of October 1943 he wrote:

> I shouldn't be wasting my time reading Russian at the moment, but I can't help it. Every time I leave it for long I feel a great nostalgia. I didn't know it was possible to fall so completely for a foreign language. All the Slav languages are good, but beside Russian, Polish and Czech seem nervous and restless,

Bulgarian poor and untutored, and Serbo-Croat, which is probably the next most satisfactory, just a little barbarous - a fine language for guerillas and men who drink slivovitz in the mountains, not yet fitted for the complex philosophies of our times. But Russian is a sad, powerful language and flows gently off the tongue like molten gold.

And, in December when he knew the mission ahead of him:

Bulgarian, I find to my delight, as far as reading it goes, is another of those languages like Italian that is handed one on a plate. It is simply Russian as a Turk would talk it - a surly Turk who wasn't sure his false teeth were going to stay in place.

Nor was this linguistic virtuosity merely technical: each assault on a new language was accompanied by an assault on the literature and history of that nation. His letters record, week after week, the novels and histories which he absorbed in this strange extra-mural self-education, and also his reflections on them.

My respect, indeed my awe, in the face of my older brother's gifts may easily be understood. Moreover, by some mystery of inheritance which I cannot explain, all the linguistic genes which descended in superabundance upon my brother were exhausted when it came to my turn. I have never been able to command a single language with any facility. My failure was evident very early in the same robust elite preparatory school in which proficiency in Greek and Latin was the only benchmark of scholastic excellence. I was not proficient. I was indeed so resistant to these languages that each term I forgot what I had been taught the term before. I did not even reach the top form. It was recognised on all sides, and most of all by myself, that I was the family duffer. But the indulgence of parents and friends allowed certain compensations; at least I was reasonably good at rough sports, like rugger, which Frank was not. And from this there flowed

50

the contradiction of our relationship. Admiring my older brother as I did, yet I felt that he needed protection in all practical matters, and that I was his protector. He had been ill in infancy in India, and from that time until perhaps his twenty-second year he never quite seemed to catch up on his own strength. As a schoolboy he was tall and thin, his head a little too large for due proportions, his limbs not exactly responsive to his control. He was notorious, until his very last year or two, for his accident-prone passage through the world - breaking things, knocking things off tables, collapsing chairs. As late as May 1943 he commented in a letter home 'Thompson is not popular in the mess at the moment - last night I broke a chair while telling a Russian joke'. At that robust, brutal and nasty preparatory school he was the kind of boy who became the butt of bullies and I, too little to protect him, would intervene with flailing fists and tears. He bore his own clumsiness philosophically and often turned it into comedy, but I, his younger brother, could not be philosophical at all. Let one anecdote do for all. One pre-war summer our parents sent us together for a week on the Norfolk Broads where we were to be instructed into how to manage a sail-boat. He was perhaps fifteen, I eleven. Our instructor one day set us a task, to splice together two ends of rope to be presented at the next day's lesson. I laboured long and dexterously and succeeded in presenting a competent splice. Frank offered a loose plaiting, mocked up in the previous five minutes, which came apart at once in the instructor's hands. The instructor, of course, commended me and went on, with unneccessary heaviness to rebuke Frank for doing so much more poorly than his little brother. I was covered utterly with confusion, which I remember to this day; here was I, my brother's protector, bringing shame upon the person I wanted so much to protect.

If anecdotes are code, then this anecdote must serve to

explain the ambiguity of our relationship. Frank did not need my protection; he didn't like games, he didn't care about splicing and his head was probably deep in Theocritus or Horace. But I felt this mixture of respect and protective concern, and I feel it still. I have no need to do so. In his last year or two in the Middle East all his faculties came at length into proportion and he showed, in the last months of his life, astonishing physical control and endurance.

We differed in other ways, not only in abilities but also in our intellectual cultures. Frank was trained within an ancient, elite, classical culture which is to me inaccessible. Frank was a scholar at Winchester, which had perhaps the highest and most rigorous classical training of any English public school. I, by contrast, attended a minor public school, founded by John Wesley with no elite pretensions and no classical ambitions. Moreover, this classical culture was, with Frank, wholly internalised. How it became internalised I understand incompletely, since it is beyond my own experience. I think that I always resented Winchester and regarded it as an influence which divided us. I did not like its self-satisfied sense of its own excellence, its cult of eccentricity and affectations, nor the ruling-class manners and arrogance of one or two of Frank's Winchester friends. My own political and cultural drive was already more low-brow, moralising - perhaps even Methodistical - and self-consciously demotic. It was therefore with delight, and with a sense of coming to terms after many years with an obstinate problem, that I read Freeman Dyson's generous account of Frank in his book *Disturbing the Universe*:

> From him I caught my first inkling of the great moral questions of war and peace that were to dominate our lives ever afterward. Listening to him talking, I learned that there is no way to rightly grasp these great questions except through poetry. For him poetry was no mere intellectual amusement.

Poetry was man's best effort down the ages to distill some wisdom from the inarticulate depths of his soul. Frank could no more live without poetry than I could live without mathematics.[1]

This is a fine definition. It is not to say that Frank's apprehension of the world and of values was aesthetic, whereas mine was (like that of the majority) more moralistic. There is something in that, certainly in our early years; but poetry was for Frank, 'no mere intellectual amusement', it was also a dimension of perception. The poetry, and the civilisations, of Greece and of Rome coloured his perception of the present and formed the ground of value - as well as a whole field for the play of reminiscence - which offered perspective to the predicament of Europe in World War Two. On the eve of the Sicilian landings in May 1943 he wrote to Iris Murdoch - who most among his correspondents shared this same sense of the co-existence of classical myth and history within the present - 'I want to talk to you about Greeks, because they are staunch anti-fascists, because they are simply among the best people I have met, because they are very much the same as the Greeks who fought at Scamander and Marathon, drove their chariots by the weeping firs on the Hill of Kronos or packed the slopes of the Acropolis to hear the Agamemnon.' And of the Sicilian landing itself he entered in his diary for the fifth of July:

> I had known our destination officially since 5th June, and unofficially, from various clues I collected, about three weeks before that. For me, of course, it provoked a host of associations. Pindar's eulogies to the tyrants of Syracuse and Akragas. Aeschylus' grave at Gela, where the Americans were

1   Freeman Dyson, *Disturbing the Universe* (London, 1981) p.35.

53

to land. The fate of that earlier army that tried to take Syracuse, our first big objective. Balaustion's recitation. Virgil's 'Trinacria' and the funeral games for Anchises. Old Frederick making a monkey of the Pope from his cool gardens in Palermo, Theocritus, Matthew Arnold...

In his correspondence with Iris Murdoch classical reference could serve as a code, to evade the military censorship and also as a form of play. This 'play' harked back to his year at New College from 1938 to 1939, a year I know little about. It was a year of anguish, passion and commitment, blended with comedy, drinking bouts and elaborate Oxford humorous affectations. It was a year of intertwined personal and political passion and commitment. Politically it commenced with Chamberlain's betrayal of Czechoslovakia at Munich and, in October of 1938 with a hard-fought bye-election battle in Oxford between a flamboyant and ill-mannered supporter of Chamberlain, Mr. Quentin Hogg, and an anti-Munich popular front candidate, A.D. Lindsay, Master of Balliol.[1] Frank's active participation as a supporter of Lindsay in this election, and the issue it raised of a European alliance against fascism led to his joining the Communist Party early in 1939. In some 'Snapshots of Oxford' which he wrote in October 1940, he recalled the disappointment of the Lindsay supporters:

> We felt glum that night at the Hollywell gate. The October air should have been a stimulus, but we were like rags soaked in cold vinegar. Obscurantism had triumphed. Some one grew bitter 'I hope North Oxford gets the first bombs. But it would

1   Mr Hogg is, of course, now better known by his inherited title as Lord Hailsham, prominent Conservative Party spokesman and jurist.

be tough on the pekineses.' Michael looked fiercely at the ground, pulled his collar up round his neck as if it was a gown, and made a pronouncement 'There are only two alternatives now - to join the Communist Party or abdicate from politics. I can't swallow communism so I'll abdicate and take up psychology '.

The personal history I can read only dimly; Frank and Iris Murdoch were part of a small, intensely self-conscious, intensely intellectual group of friends, each of whom in series, appeared to be in a state of unrequited, desperate and voluble passion for each other. Every one seemed to have been in love with the wrong person. Some of the story is told in the 'Snapshots'. In spite of his friend's pronouncement, Frank did not seriously consider joining the Communist Party until the following Spring. He left the Liberal Club 'because it was so frivolous', but 'knew enough about Labour leaders to have no use for them either'.

When Iris Murdoch suggested 'What about the Communist Party?' he recalled that he was 'dumbstruck', but invited her to 'come to tea in a couple of days and convert me'. The conversion was accomplished, but in the summer of 1939 every one in the country was in a state of nervous tension. It was not a good time to be obsessed with personal relationships 'That was a bad passage the first fortnight of the summer term', he wrote, 'like something in rather poor taste from de Musset. I was pining green for Iris, who was gently sympathetic but not at all helpful. Michael was lashing himself into a frenzy for Leonie who would draw him on and then let him down with a thud. In the evenings we would swap sorrows and read bits of Verlaine to each other. I must have spent three whole days walking round and round the garden, in intervals between writing her letters which I tore up...'

Frank's still-adolescent poems of the summer of 1939 are full of the self-dramatising melancholy of rejection. Yet this unrequited obsession proved to be, as evidenced in subsequent years of correspondence, the foundation for a close and increasingly tender friendship. As the years of correspondence went on, the recruit seemed to become more committed to a communist cause, the recruiter less committed. I say 'a' and not 'the' communist cause, since Frank Thompson can scarcely be defined as an orthodox communist.

This is perhaps a matter which we should explore a little further. Nothing appears more sinister to Mr Laurence Martin and other authors whose work sometimes appears from a neighbouring institute, than the fact that there were British communists sent as liaison officers to aid resistance movements, some even at work within intelligence units like SOE. A part of this question I will discuss later. But it seems useful at this point to define a little further what, in 1939-40, this Communist commitment was. The basis for the commitment lay in an internationalist anti-fascist contestation, in an era of Western ruling-class appeasement, non-intervention (but effective complicity with reaction) in Spain, tenacious and oppressive imperial rule in the dependencies of all the imperialist nations, racial segregation and oppression in the United States, and in all countries ruling-class inertia in the face of depression, unemployment and severe social hardship of every kind. 'The Left', far more than any other section of opinion understood, publicised and opposed the advance of Nazism and Fascism, and the persecution of Jews, intellectuals and oppositionists of all kinds in Germany and Italy and parts of the Balkans. One pole of the commitment found positive strong identification with the Government forces in Spain and with the International Brigades where such British Communists as Ralph Fox, Christopher Caudwell and John Cornford had already given their lives, and, in a more cloudy and self-deceiving way, with a Utopian construct known as 'the Soviet Union'.

The international fraternity, then, was with the anti-fascist opposition in Europe, in Horthy's jails, in German concentration camps, in Bulgarian police cells, on Italian prison islands or hemmed in in the last strongholds of Republican Spain. The Communist party was seen, first of all, as the universal organiser of resistance, with a discipline tough enough to withstand that incredibly rigorous persecution. It was also seen as the main organiser of frontal contestation with Britain's home-grown fascists, Mosley's Blackshirts. I am not here attempting any analysis or critique, nor apologetics; I am simply attempting to recover what the overt commitments of those times were, and also what they were not. The commitment to something called Communism was political and internationalist. In Britain at least it entailed, from the late thirties to the mid-forties, rather little commitment to any doctrinal orthodoxies. Although British communists, around the journal *Left Review* sometimes engaged in Marxist discourse, their Marxist credentials have been ridiculed subsequently by orthodox Marxists of most complexions. There are few references to Marx or Marxism in Frank Thompson's letters, and more than one of these is ironic.

There is also a peculiar notion to be found in some recent academic writing, that adherence to communism entailed a set of conspiratorial activities, membership of 'cells' permeating this or that organisation. On this matter I can speak with a little authority. Frank Thompson's organised relationship with the communist party must have been slight and have lasted for only about six months. He was a member of the Oxford University branch and also of the Oxford University Labour Club; on vacations and leaves he had some brief association, political discussions, selling the *Daily Workers,* with the very small home branch at Princes Risborough. Communists who were serving in the armed forces were normally not in any organised association, they did not even hold membership cards and many, over the years, drifted out of any allegiance to the party. There were not, to my knowledge, any communist cells in the British armed forces: perhaps, on occasion, there ought to have been. Sometimes individual communists would find each other out and, in association with other left-wingers, set up, in base areas, discussion groups, wall newspapers and other educational and informational activities. Such groups and activities of Communists, Labour Party members and others can be traced within the famous Forces' Parliament in Cairo and in the strikes and near-mutinies among the British troops in India after the war. I wholly applaud these activities.

I was a Communist in the armed forces myself, and can say that I know of no evidence that Frank Thompson had any organised contact with the Communist Party of Great Britain from the time that he left England in March 1941 until the time of his death. That is to say, no action of his followed on 'instructions' from King Street or from the Comintern.

I am not here arguing, in any way, that Frank was not, by commitment, a Communist. I am seeking to recover what, in terms of the years 1939 to 1940 and in terms of his own personality, this commitment was, and to rescue the notion from the stereotypes deriving from subsequent Cold War projections. And we may note that his life conforms uneasily with stereotypes of either discipline or doctrine. To volunteer for the services on the outbreak of war was not upon any Party instructions, for in the eyes of the British Communist Party that war, until the Soviet Union was attacked, remained an 'imperialist' war, to which the proper response was revolutionary defeatism.

This last point might be evaded by special pleading. It is true that for the first ten days or so, the British Communist Party did endorse the war as potentially 'anti-fascist'. What happened (I have been told) is that in the days before the declaration of war the British Communist leadership, percipient enough to realise that dramatic events were impending, set up a commission of four to consult daily with the editor of the *Daily Worker* and to ensure that it followed a correct editorial line. On the day of the war's commencement the commission had met and under its instructions the editor had indicted a neat editorial appraising the German ultimatum to Poland, finding Herr Hitler's terms to be not unreasonable, and recommending the Poles to accept. The editor, William Rust, then packed up his dispatch case and he and the rest of the commission's members proceeded by tube trains to their separate suburban homes, leaving as night editor in charge of the paper the literary editor, Randall Swingler, a poet, an editor of *Left Review* who was also more genuinely anti-fascist and a better political thinker than any of that august commission. As the deadline for the press approached, Swingler glancing idly at the incoming ticker-tape noted with alarm that German tanks had crossed the frontier into Poland. He tried without effect to contact any of the members of the high commission, but each was in his separate stretch of the suburban subway. He ran down, stopped the presses and, on the stone, wrote out a defiant editorial committing the paper (and the movement) to support of the war, concluding 'This is a war which can and must be won.' He was met on the next morning with grave faces and grave rebukes; how could a poet determine the political line of the Party? But the Party, none the less, was committed. Ten days later David Springhall, the British courier to the Comintern in Moscow, arrived back in London. It had been overlooked that war in central Europe would disrupt all rail transport, and he had been forced to take a slow passage through the Baltic. In Springhall's briefcase were quite contrary instructions; Pollitt temporarily resigned from secretaryship of the CPGB and the war was proclaimed to be an imperialist one after all.

This anecdote may also be read as code, signalling the confusions and mixed motives of that time in the aftermath of the Molotov-Ribbentrop pact. I cannot confirm it since the participants - that High Party Commission, William Rust, the editor, David Springhall and my friend and informant, Randall Swingler, are now all dead. But the switch in the line did indeed take place. Should it then be assumed that Frank Thompson volunteered for the army in the enthusiasm of the first (anti-fascist war) line and, when the line changed, was already irrevocably enlisted ? No, it cannot. For my parents, in an exercise of intervention of a kind from which I was also occasionally to suffer, brought pressure to bear, both through college authorities and through the War Office, to secure Frank's release on the grounds of his youth and incompleted studies, which release was indeed obtained. In stormy scenes the release was rejected. Among his papers I find a trace of this argument, directed not at his parents but 'To Madonna Bolshevichka', dated October 1939:

> Sure, lady, I know the party line is better.
> I know what Marx would have said. I know you're right.
> When this is over we'll fight for the things that matter.
> Somehow, today, I simply want to fight.
> That's heresy? Okay. But I'm past caring.
> There's blood about my eyes, and mist and hate.
> I know the things we're fighting now and loathe them.
> Now's not the time you say ? But I can't wait
>
> Maybe I'm not so wrong. Maybe tomorrow
> We'll meet again. You'll smile and you'll agree.
> And *then* we'll raise revolt and blast the heavens.
> But now there's only one course left for me.

Across this Frank wrote, before he left for the Middle East, BILGE, but whether this indicated a rejection of the self-dramatisation, or of the poetics or the political line of the

60

poem I cannot tell. In 1940, during the phoney war, there is a clear decline in Frank's belief that the British government had the least commitment to any but national and imperial interests. The poems of that year have a very different tone, for example 'London 1940', written after the Blitz had begun, and dated in October of that year:

> After fourteen hours clearing they came to him
> Under the twisted girders and the rubble.
> They would not let me see his face.
> Now I sit shiftlessly on the tube platforms
> Or huddle, a little tipsy, in brick-built shelters.
> I can see with an indifferent eye
> The red glare over by the docks and hear
> Impassively the bomb-thuds in the distance.
>
> For me, a man with not many interests
> And no pretensions to fame, that was my world,
> My son of fifteen, my only concrete achievement,
> Whom they could not protect. Stepping aside
> From the Great Crusade, I will play the idiot's part.
> You, if you like, may wave your fists and crash
> On the wrong doorsteps brash retaliation.

Nevertheless, writing home from Egypt in 1941, he recalled the periods of duty in England when an invasion seemed imminent, 'when the news from France trickled through and one tried to realise that those free and friendly Sussex fields were hardly more than thirty miles from the anger of the Reichswehr...' and reckoned that that year 'starting from the invasion of Norway, will count as one of the most memorable in the island's history.' If this is all to argue that Frank does not conform with the stereotypes of communist discipline, he conforms even less to stereotypes of doctrine. Repeatedly, in his letters, he offers to humanise Communist doctrine, sometimes indeed to the point of glossing over it. Within his

61

general anti-fascist commitment which, as the war went on, was increasingly embodied in the gigantic feats of the Red Army and of the communist-led resistance movements in Europe he situated his judgement in concrete historical and personal locations rather than in a priori abstractions. His letters dicuss, for example, the fate of Polish landowners banished to work camps beyond the Urals, trying to sort out propaganda on both sides from actuality, and condemning gratuitous cruelty to individuals, even where wartime conditions and the exigencies of Nazi conquest made the justice available rough at best:

> But, most important of all, in a world as filthy as it is today one should remember how helpless and how lonely the individual human being is; and that kindliness, especially when it costs so little, is a policy that justifies itself...

One should add also that Frank Thompson remained a Wykehamist: that curious freemasonry of self-assured intellectuals was a class elite to which he, willy-nilly belonged. He did not simply belong to an elite of Officers as opposed to Other Ranks, but to an elite of special persons within the Officers. Throughout his years of overseas service encounters with fellow Wykehamists go on - 'The other day I met Evans-Pritchard, anthropologist, old Wykehamist... Together we drank arak and watched a French general dancing with his mistress, talked most about Winchester, but a little also about the decline of Western Europe, the coming ascendency of Asia...' No doubt his Wykehamist credentials gave him rather more choice of the work he did than would have come to the generality of officers. They may indeed have helped him to get transferred in the summer of 1940 from the Artillery to the elite GHQ Liaison Regiment then in formation, where some of his fellow-officers came from even more rarified social heights. He wrote in one letter home 'Michael

Astor's patrol has had a good time. Today he went out pheasant shooting and took them as beaters.'

Feelings about his fellow-officers were ambiguous. On the one hand, he shared a military comradeship with them and often paid tribute to their courage and efficiency. Indeed when I wrote to him making some jibes about a Harrovian fellow-trainee I received something of a rebuke:

> ...I think it is salutary to remember that these chaps, even your co-trainees who seem so childish, often make brave and even efficient soldiers...there's no getting away from the fact that the regiments whose officers are the most blue-blooded - the Guards, old cavalry regiments - have proved themselves among the best fighting regiments in the British Army...

On the other hand, their lack of curiosity, their complete lack of interest in the people of the countries in which they were stationed appalled him. He wrote home from Cairo in March 1943:

> I think I may have been unfair in some of my recent letters to our officer class. There are tremendous reserves of energy here, if only they could be harnessed to the war effort. One of our officers, for instance, has compiled a complete form-book for the local races - forty pages plus an impeccable index-system. And last night when I returned to the mess after midnight, I found two other brother-officers huddled over the lamp checking and re-checking the scores for the evening's session of poker.

In his Sicilian diary an officer who had, though wounded himself stayed to help the other wounded rather than take the chance of leaving the action, received the compliment - 'A very gallant gentleman, even for a Grenadier Guard.'

In general his fellow officers were judged by their actions, though there were certainly traces of respect for social status as well. But snob or not, he was first and foremost an intellectual. He found it easier, I suspect, to converse in Polish, Greek or Russian with fellow-intellectuals in the Middle East than in English with soldiers of the British working class. This may simply be because his European acquaintances made better copy in his letters. For example, 'Z':

> This afternoon I went for a long walk with my old friend Z—, the interpreter whom I used to know in Persia. In a strange mixture of Russian and Polish we reviewed Polish politics of the last twenty-five years, the tragic assassination of Narutowic, the 'guided democracy' (lovely expression) of Pilsudski, the banning of Sikorski from Pilsudski's funeral and the pigheadedness of Lithuanians. Then he began to explain and illustrate the theory of Polish dancing. This vast and moon-faced man of forty, ludicrous at any time in battle-dress, suddenly beginning dancing hornpipes on a muddy lane between palm-groves...

But his attititude to 'other ranks' remained in some respects Wykehamical, affectionately paternalist:

This is the third day of the *khamsin*,
The fierce monotonous insistence
Of hot dry blast, silting up eyes and hair,
Taut-straining the frayed guy-ropes of resistance.
Heat thick enough to cut. Wind but no air.
Two swaddies pitching tent in the full sun,
Tugging the bellying canvas down,
Stripped to the waist, hair matted, eyes, back, chest
Caked in a sweaty plaster, shake their heads.
'Well Bill? Yer glad yer came out East ?'
'Ho, yuss! I wouldn't have missed this for quids!'

Oh England! Oh my lovely casual country!
These are your lads, English as blackthorn-flower,
Bearing your freshness with them, facing each hour,
Desert or death, with the same free unstudied

Serenity of meadowland in April -
Carelessly littered with fritillaries,
Ladysmock, kingcups, cowslips and wild apple!

It was a strange military society in which he lived for
three years, perhaps more various than is always remembered.
He wrote in May 1941 'Even the Roman Empire never flooded
Egypt with a horde like the present'. A year later, in August
1942 he described some of its make-up:

There is something epic about this 'Middle East' if only one
could get a frame for it. We have an assortment of nationalities
that would make Caesar's legions look like a team from the
Home Counties. The Russians, driving north through Hamadan,
close-cropped, berry-brown, in dark blue breeches with
knee-boots, grinning fit to bust and giving the V-sign to every
one they pass; the diminutive Iraquis in khaki breeches and
puttees mounting guard among the white hollyhocks on the
Persian frontier; the Arab legion and the French *meharistes*,
slender and almost girlish in their red-and-white *kefiyehs* and
long brown cassocks, camps like old Tamurlane on the green
steppe-land, swaying round the fire in dances that might have
come from *Sanders of the River*; Indians everywhere, the
neatest, cleanest and most dignified soldiers in our army - fat,
bearded Sikhs, P.M.s with their pointed puggarees, and
Gurkhas (are those Gurkhas with their almost Malayan
features?) travelling impassively on the backs of trucks; coons
everywhere, squatting round brush-fires, driving down main
roads like a wind out of hell, grinning in road-gangs, but never,
that I could see, working (on the Phoenician sea coast a camp
with a large crocodile mosaicked out in white pebbles with the
word BASUTOLAND); elegant Greek and Yugoslav officers
preening themselves on the streets of Alex; Fighting French,
Poles, Canucks, Yanks in jeeps, huge South Africans almost
childlike in their docility, New Zealanders, rough-hewn and
intelligent, Aussies, rough-hewn and undoubtedly villainous.
And Englishmen? Yes, there are quite a few Englishmen -

nearly always to be recognised by their utter civilianity, the complete lack of martial fire or any other eccentricity with which they stroll down streets and stare wistfully into shop windows. And glimpses, not always without humour, of the Wops and Dutchies. This war is demonstrating, beyond any hope of refutation, the Unity of Man. No one, at least, who's been in the Middle East will want to deny it...

The work in this theatre was only episodic. The work of his liaison unit took him from the Western Desert to Iran and from Sinai to Sicily. Action was interspersed with routine maintenance and training exercises, and also wide sweeps through the Near East - Iraq, Jordan, Beirut - gathering intelligence. It is not an easy environment to rediscover today. We know what an army was from books, films and TV serials; but this was not that kind of army. We know, too, the anti-heroic image of *Catch 22*, yet it was not that kind of army either. The British army of the Western Desert dispensed with much of the outward form of military discipline, sometimes even of uniforms. Yet it became a self-disciplined, highly professional formation. Increasingly civilian in character, it refused the ostentatious display of military hierarchy or rhetoric by means of collective irony. Frank noted in his diary on 6th July, on the eve of the Sicilian landing:

> ...the Brigadier addressed all troops of the 151 Bde in one of the mess decks. A short, competent speech, stressing the need for alertness and good communications. Ended with the words 'Think to yourselves you're fit, you know your job, you've got guts and you're the 151 Brigade Group. If any one can think of any better reasons than that for why we're going to win, I'd like him to come and tell me. Right-ho! See you on the beaches.' I thought myself it was a good speech, but I heard a grumble from behind me 'On the beaches will he? Bloody early he'll be on the beaches, I'll bet.' No malice. Simply the formal and legitimate registration of a protest...

66

Irony is the point at which one should start if one is to anatomise that half military, half civilian culture. Yet it was rarely a mode that Frank Thompson used. The contest for the Western Desert stirred in him Homeric recollections and reviewing it in retrospect he signed off the history in epic dimensions:

> It looks as though the desert may be cleared up this winter. For a while it will still see Allied troops, but sooner or later these are bound to leave. The furrowed tracks that were once as busy as Oxford Street will be covered over with sand. The burnt-out vehicles and planes will be picked clean by the Senyussi. The wooden crosses, except for those in the coastal cemeteries, will fade and rot in the rain. But as long as our generation is alive, the Libyan desert will not be forgotten. For several years it gave us a home and was not unduly hostile. It has been enriched by some of the finest deeds of courage and endurance in man's history. As deserts go it is a good desert, and all of us who served there are proud of the memory.

The irony of the general soldiery in World War II had a different edge to it from that of World War I. In the first war it was bitter, sometimes defeatist, savagely resistant to the rhetoric of war. In the second it was wittier, more selective in its targets and those targets were less the war itself than the manners and rhetoric of upper-class officers and of military bureaucracy in general. Beneath the ironic commentary was a deeper assent to the necessity of the war itself - indeed sometimes an assent to changing its direction and infusing into it a greater democratic content than some subsequent accounts, coloured by the hindsight given by Yalta and the later betrayals, by both sides, of the Cold War, have allowed. It was this assent and these aims which are voiced in Frank Thompson's letters containing as they do barely a hint of irony. The epic to which he had been committed from the first moment of his enlistment, had been that of the liberation of

67

Europe from fascist occupation and fascist repression. 'With the fate of centuries being fought out around Kalinin and Mozhaisk, I feel like a grasshopper singing in a thunderstorm' he wrote in October 1941. In November '...the sacrifices of the Russians make Coventry and London look like a couple of train accidents'. In the same month he wrote in a letter home:

> Aren't the Slavs a splendid lot? The Poles have suffered more than any nation in Europe. The Czechs, especially their students, have done far better than we had any right to expect. I try to imagine myself standing in Broad Street while the officials of the National Union of Students are shot in cold blood. That's what happened in Prague. Serb rebels are currently reported to be in virtual control of a quarter of Serbia. Perhaps it's not just coincidence that Serb resistance has been much stronger since Russia came in. There's a strong Communist movement in Yugoslavia. Even the old peasant Bulgars will turn in the end - just you see. Nor is it the first time the Slavs have thrown their bodies between Europe and destruction. They bore the brunt of the Turks and the Tartars too. 'To suffer like a Slav' will soon become a by-word in all the world's languages...

Perhaps his situation in a GHQ intelligence-gathering unit enabled him to have earlier knowledge of the growth of a European resistance than was general at that time. In January 1942 he wrote:

> I think we should soft-pedal the 'Britain can take it' stuff. We have only to think what the Poles, Czechs, Norwegians, Serbs, Greeks, Dutch, French, Belgians and people of occupied Russia are suffering at this moment, to realise how unjustly fortunate we've been up to now.

And in June, (to Iris Murdoch):

> At the moment I feel only shame - shame that, while Russians are dying at Kharkov and my own countrymen facing living

hell beneath the Libyan dogstar, I am in another part of the Middle East with nothing to fear but scorpions.

And in the next month:

> Oh, where is this second front Irushka? Do people at home realise that if Russia goes we shall have to fight back from the Americas? Do they realise how long this would take, if, indeed, it is possible at all?

Iris, writing back, lamented her war work in the Treasury:

> I would volunteer for anything that would be certain to take me abroad. Unfortunately…the Treasury would never let me go… Sometimes I think it's quite bloody being a woman. So much of one's life has to consist of having an attitude.

Even the weather was closely watched for its signal in this European epic. He wrote from Iran in September 1942:

> day before yesterday we saw a cloud no bigger than a man's hand gazing at us thoughtfully from his O.P. above the hills to the north-east. Yesterday when we went down to the river we looked across at the Tall Mountain of Precipices. Around his head and flaking off to the low western hills was a party of clouds that had come to make a reconnaissance in force. Messages from our outlying patrols speak of encounters with cold rain and thunderstorms - 'Weather breaking soon. Weather breaking.' And all of us - not that we love rain in these surroundings - are glad of the news of it. At the cookhouse, in the fitter's shop, in the small canteen tent where we gather for the evenings, men look with relief and gratitude to the coming rain. Rain here will mean rain at Mozdok and at Tuapse. Rain here will mean rain on all the approaches to Stalingrad. Rain here will mean rain at Voronezh, Orel and Kalinin. Rain here will mean rain, and shortly snow, on the roads that lead from Viborg, Riga, Vilno and hard-pressed Leningrad. Rain here will mean the descent of Arctic winter on all the approaches to Murmansk and Archangelsk. To the Bolsheviks a respite. To

the United Nations, if they use it well, a turning-point.

It was in Iran that he began to follow regularly the news bulletins on Russian radio, from which he learnt much about the European resistance which went unreported in the West. 'It was only when I tuned in to Radio Moscow last night that I heard how a hundred and sixteen Frenchmen had been executed in France as a result of the Valmy day demonstrations.' By January 1943 he was giving educational lectures on occupied Europe. On 2nd June he wrote in his diary:

> This nineteen hundred and forty-third year of grace is going to be a great year to live or die in. It can only be compared to the end of the Ice Age, when the glaciers receded and restored to Europe her freedom. That took millenia and this may be a matter of months.

But later that summer, after the Sicilian landings, the theme began to take a more sombre, personal note. On 26 July he wrote home from Malta:

> Every one just now is exulting about Mussolini. My chief regret is that Geoffrey Garratt is not here to enjoy and record this last chapter of his story.[1] It's more than ever necessary now, with this wave of self-righteousness spreading over British propaganda, with the First and Eighth armies wearing

1   Geoffrey Garratt, close friend of E.J. Thompson and co-author with him of *Rise and Fulfilment of British Rule in India* (London, Macmillan 1934) had also written a popular Penguin on *Mussolini's Roman Empire*, opposing the appeasement of fascism. Professor E.F. Carritt and his wife Winifred were neighbours whose sons had grown up with Frank and Edward. One son, Anthony, had died in the Spanish Civil War.

Crusader's shields, with the Church doing its level best to corner the moral credit for the war on Fascism, to remember those men who, in the sierras and on the banks of the Ebro, bore the heat of the day alone; who fought against hopeless odds, while many of our leading churchmen were expressing delight that the trains ran to time in fascist Italy. This is their victory - Cornford's victory, Ralph Fox's victory, the victory of the Carritts and the Garratts, of the Asturian miners and Barcelona working men. Those of us who came after were merely adopting an idea that they proved - that freedom and Fascism can't live in the same world, and that the free man, once he realises this, will always win.

The failure of the West to open a second front he felt with an almost personal sense of shame; he wrote in August '...in five or six weeks, unless I've read the bird's entrails wrong, the Nazis will have moved twenty or thirty divisions from Western Europe and that (Russian) drive which might have freed Warsaw this year will be slowed down. Thank God for the Bulgars and the Danes who seem to be providing at least something of a diversion.'

It was at this point that Frank succeeded in transferring from GHQ liaison to the work of SOE. The move requires no conspiratorial theory of either Wykehamist influences or Communist penetration to explain it. It is transparently clear from his own writing in his diaries and letters that he felt he belonged in the European resistance movement. His qualifications for such work were outstanding. How many other servicemen in the Middle East commanded seven or eight European languages, had battle experience in the Western Desert and in Sicily and had served for over a year as second in command of an elite signals and intelligence unit? He wrote in October 1943 'A chemical change is taking place in Europe which few outsiders understand... When German Fascism falls, reaction will have lost its strongest prop.

Nothing this side of the Atlantic will be strong enough to buttress it again.' Having found the course which he wanted to take, he began to see himself, almost as if from outside, as an instrument of liberation. An arduous course of parachute training left him with a great admiration for the courage of the regular parachute troops for whom the jump was an immediate prelude to savage fighting. He knew he would not face the prospect of jumping without fear, but that nevertheless he would face it. He wrote:

> If it were necessary would I go through that course again? I hope very much I shall always be able to do what is necessary. I should approach it in far less nonchalant a mood. In any case, there are no two ways about it. Any rifle is useless until it has been zeroed. Any sword is just a slice of junk until it has been tempered. In the same way a man - and every man is a weapon in this fight, which will only end when we achieve some mythical perfection - sooner or later must be tried. My tempering has only just begun, but I mean the process to be thorough.

The training did not, however, lead on, as he had hoped it would to early service as a liaison officer with the Greek partisans. Instead he found himself temporarily employed at a desk in the headquarters of SOE in Cairo, in the Greek section:

> So I go on, he wrote, and the Russians, so they say, are fighting like Bogatyrs east of Zhitomir. There are times when I hate this present temporary job with a more active, 'dynamic' hatred than I can ever recollect feeling for a job before. But it has compensations. It brings me constantly in contact with a people whom I have long known to be among the most delightful, though also the most infuriating, in the world. And it is educating me. Things which before I had only grasped theoretically I now know with my eyes and ears and with the black reservoir of anger which lies at the back of the brain and sometimes roars in deluge over the whole of it.

72

What he had come to learn at the Greek desk was the character of British policies towards the Greek partisans. On the first of December he wrote to Iris Murdoch:

I have been stripped of my few remaining illusions in the last year (I speak solely of political illusions), and harbour now a great deal of malice towards some. I have lost altogether the pseudo-heroic mood I had three months ago when I first volunteered for parachute duties. I still press for more active work because it seems to suit my temperament better than sitting in an office, but I don't worry overmuch. If they choose to keep me at base now my training's over, they may. I feel it won't be a tragedy if I survive the war. I can see so many evil men and so many myriads of petty men surviving well-entrenched and I don't think that I, for all my manifest vices, am either of these. I believe that every man of good will is going to be badly needed in the years that lie ahead. But for all that, I would rather now be on the Sangro river - I know that for certain, and don't say it to reassure you nor even myself...

At Christmas a party of Yugoslav partisans came to confer in Cairo and he wrote:

With the passing of the year I seem to have come to a watershed in my life. I have had some profoundly moving experiences. I have had the honour to meet and talk to some of the best people in the world people whom, when the truth is known, Europe will recognise as among the finest and toughest she has ever borne. Meeting them has made me utterly disgusted with some aspects of my present life, reminding me forcibly that all my waking hours should be dedicated to one purpose only... Nothing else matters. We must crush the Nazis and build our whole life anew. 'If we should meet again, why then we'll smile.' If not, why then those that follow us will be able to smile far more happily and honestly in the world that we all helped to make...

We have now come to the eve of his departure to Serbia.

When I consider these late letters and the last months of his life there is a contrast in experience (when set beside today's undergraduate and graduate students in Britain and the United States) which must already have suggested itself. Yet I still find it difficult to realise that Frank Thompson was only twenty-three. Of course this was in the character of his times. The resistance movement in Europe was a movement of the young. Colonel Dencho Znepolski, the military commander of the Second Sofia Brigade was the same age as Frank. Now we spin out the business of coming to maturity much longer, sometimes far too long. The conditions of those times made for a forced development, a premature maturity. Yet even among contemporary colleagues in the Middle East there were many who expressed astonishment when they learned his age. He was not only a competent and confident commander in military action, but also seems, in any company, to have been taken as the philosopher and historian of the party.

And yet, as he suggested himself sometimes, this forced growth may have been made possible only by the loss of other possibilities and capacities for experience. The long and colourful letters contain little self-examination. In February 1942 he had written:

> Very rarely now do I find myself inspecting the murky mass of incoherence which a metaphysician would call my 'soul'. My chief intellectual interests are in the earth and the people on it, especially the 'characters', and in myself as a potential 'character' in the figure that I cut to the outside world - a figure which probably bears no relation to the one I would find 'in the silences of my own mind'.

His letters also, especially those to Iris Murdoch, lamented the monotonous masculinity of military culture.

All these themes, and indeed several of the themes of this lecture, came together in his last letter to Iris Murdoch written on 21st April 1944 from Tergoviste in Southern Serbia. It will be recalled that for the previous three months, since he had dropped out of the skies into the snows of Dobro Polje, he had been ceaselessly on the move, hunted from camp to camp, had lost his colleague Mostyn Davies and had at length found his way down to the headquarters of Tempo and Apostolski. His last letter began with an apology: 'Irushka! Sorry I haven't written for so long. Old Brotoloig seems to have been monopolising my attention.' Here again is a Homeric reference, for Homer frequently gives to Ares, the god of war, the epithet 'Brotoloigos' - plague-like or baneful to man.

In the correspondence between Iris and Frank between 1942 and 1944 there is a sense of two travellers whose respect and affection for each other remains whole and constant, but who are being drawn apart by the vessels of divergent circumstances and experience. On 17th October 1942 Frank wrote:

> Three years and a bit since I joined the army. More than that since you and I first exchanged Weltanschauungs in a room at Ruskin. Now I am twenty-two instead of eighteen and you are twenty-three, almost a matron. It looks like being another three years straight before we meet again. We shall probably find we have both changed out of all knowing and have nothing any longer in common...

In April '43 he wrote 'I'm very little of an introvert. Only when writing to you or my brother do I make an effort at introspection.' Iris wrote in October of that year 'You must be changing a great deal, and it's hard for me to measure the stuff of the change from your letters - which are in the old vein...' She herself was given more to introversial self-exploration. Her letters in the final year expressed something of the ennui of Whitehall, of her own ambitions as a writer, the conversations in the literary pubs of central London, the gathering world-weariness and political pessimism of her immediate circle and her own failing self-confidence. Such letters, parachuting into Southern Serbia brought a strange savour of an antique, half-forgotten culture. 'A good deal of talk about weariness of soul' Frank growled 'I want to hear no more of this.'

I can't think why you are so interested in MORALS. Chiefly a question of the liver and digestive organs I assure you. On one occasion when I had to go without sugar for a month I felt by the end of it as though I could have won a continence contest against Hippolytus

αμματων δ'ευ αχηυιαιυ
ερρει παο 'Αφροδιτα

Oh yes, I know this is only one small aspect of morals, but you see what I mean. And yet the question of building a new communal ethic is one of the most important that we have to elaborate. My young brother is tremendously keen on this and talks very soundly about it.

My own list of priorities is as follows

1. *People* and everything to do with people, their habits, their loves and hates, their arts, their languages. Everything of importance revolves around *people*

2. Animals and flowers. These bring me a constant undercurrent of joy. Just now I'm revelling in plum blossom and young lambs and the first leaves on the briar roses. One doesn't need any more than these. I couldn't wish for better company.

These are enough for a hundred lifetimes. And yet I must confess to being very fond of food and drink also.

I envy you and Michael in one way. All this time you are doing important things like falling in and out of love - things which broaden and deepen and strengthen the character more surely than anything else. I can honestly say I've never been in love. When I pined for you I was too young to know what I was doing - no offence meant. Since then I haven't lost an hour's sleep over any of Eve's daughters. This means I'm growing up lop-sided, an overgrown boy. Ah well, - I shall find time, Cassius, I shall find time.

All the same, I don't think you should fall for 'emotional fascists' - Try to avoid that...

As in many of his letters, especially to Murdoch, there are two letters to be read here. the apparent letter offers himself as 'a character' - robustly resistant to self-examination, blunt, driving hard towards positives. The other letter, unwritten but implied, is harder in tone, harder to interpret. It refers to the old code of the 'Agammemnon Class' of 1939. The lines cited come from Agammemnon, 418-9. The chorus has just spoken of the 'dowry of death' which Helen had brought to Troy, and goes on to recall what the Trojan prophets had said of Menelaus:

> The agony of his loss is clear before us. Longing for her who lies beyond the sea he shall see a phantom queen in his household Her images in their beauty are bitterness to her lord now where in the emptiness of eyes all passion has failed.

The chorus continues to lament the tragedies of war:

> In all Hellas, for those who swarmed to the last the heartbreaking misery shows in the house of each. Many are they who are touched at the heart [Greek, 'liver'] by these things. Those they sent forth they knew; now, in place of the young men urns and ashes are carried to the houses of the fighters.

The reminiscence I suppose is to the battle of Comernik: the burned villages and homesteads of the Crna Trava region. Yet, with Hippolytus (and we have now left Aeschylus for

Euripides, or perhaps for Juvenal) there is an ironic counter-reference, which perhaps looks forward to the later part of the letter. For Hippolytus' dedication to chastity (and to the chase) earned only the revenge of Aphrodite for his neglect of her. 'Nay' asked Juvenal 'What profit did Hippolytus get from his stern resolution?'

The self-criticism and the self-examination is recorded. Yet it is difficult not to read the letter as a signal, across the years, of a divergent experience too great to allow for direct communication - almost as a rebuke. These months of desperate warfare, physical endurance and comradeship in extremity had displaced more personal concerns - 'in the emptiness of eyes all passion has failed.'

When many years later Iris Murdoch wrote a poem in memoriam Frank Thompson, she entitled it 'The Agamemnon Class, 1939'

> Do you remember Professor
> Eduard Fraenkel's endless
> Class of the Agamemnon ?
> Between line eighty-three and line a thousand
> It seemed to us our innocence
> Was lost, our youth laid waste,
> In that pellucid, unforgiving air...

***

> The hero's tomb is a disputed mound.
> What really happened on the windy plain?
> The young are bored by stories of the war.
> And you, the other young who stayed there
> In the land of the past are courteous and pale,
> Aloof, holding your fates.

Lecture Three

'MET Thompson on gallop', Major Saunders had signalled on 12th of May, 'He going Bulgaria'... What happened on the windy plain?

We commence with somewhat differing - although not necessarily incompatible - accounts of the state of mind of the man (or, as he had just described himself to Iris Murdoch, 'lop-sided boy') who commanded the British Mission. The first account came from fellow British officers, liaising with the Macedonians and Serbs, who talked with him in the previous three weeks. In June 1944 Major Henniker-Major wrote:

> When I saw Thompson he was tired and had, I think, done well under difficult circumstances. No one helped him from Cairo, or patted him on the back, and he was discouraged. Tempo says they should never have tried to penetrate Bulgaria before they had built up a reasonable force outside on Yugoslav territory and he fears for their safety. Thompson fully realised the dangers and possible folly of going into Bulgaria when he did. He, however, decided to take the gamble... At the present, according to Tempo, their organisation is incredibly bad.[1]

1   WO 202/164 Letter Henniker-Major 6 June 1944.

In a fuller recollection, thirty-five years later, Major
Henniker-Major wrote:

> When I met him, Frank was desperately tired - physically and
> emotionally; little wonder, after the marches, uncertainties and
> then Mostyn Davies' death and his narrow escape. So tired that
> one night when we had a move he went to sleep on the march
> and fell over a small cliff into a river... I liked him very much;
> he'd suddenly been saddled with the whole responsibility; he
> was, I think, very exhausted; he had to put up a constant fight
> to avoid being taken over by the Yugoslavs and to steer a
> middle course between this and being led off on a lunatic
> expedition by the Bulgars. I remember meeting the Bulgars
> with him and forming the impression that I was glad they were
> not my prop and stay - a pretty inexperienced and low-level
> mixture of individual deserters and Communist civilians from
> the towns... Compared to the Yugoslavs they had an unreal and
> slightly horror-comic air of a brigand army, boastful, mercurial,
> temperamental and [with] an inexperienced yen to go it alone. I
> remember thinking that Frank, though very steamed up, was
> sensible and objective... In my talks with Frank I never knew
> he was a Communist; he was far less obtrusively so than people
> I had with me at times. He seemed entirely objective. I think
> anyway that at that time we were all genuinely operating a
> non-political directive...[1]

So far from finding Frank euphoric, he found him to be
depressed; 'There was still no clear policy about what to do in
support of the Bulgarian partisans', he had little direction from
Cairo, there were scarcely any sorties of supplies, and
'probably most important - he was bloody tired and impatient
of delays.'
    Beside this we can set the rather different recollections of

1   Letter Henniker-Major (later Lord Henniker).

Djura Zlatkovic, former commander of the Crna Trava (Serbian) Partisan Brigade, which frequently provided escorts for the Mission. In his account, Thompson 'had a will to get across to Bulgaria as soon as possible' although the Yugoslav partisan leadership warned him to stay in the security of Serbian territory. In the last two days discussions took place, perhaps at Kalna, between Tempo and members of the Bulgarian partisan staff, in which Thompson took an active part. He had 'the thesis that if the British Mission went across, bringing airdrops of arms and supplies on to Bulgarian territory, this would provide a new atmosphere and would arouse mass support... Frank was self-confident - he had a hard opinion that if they got through they would get arms in and a mass uprising would take place.'[1]

I think that these accounts share parts of the truth. Frank Thompson was certainly exasperated by Cairo's lack of guidance. He also appears to have hoped that the example of practice - a partisan free territory in the heart of Bulgaria - could have raised a quite new intensity of resistance. The caution and exhaustion which he revealed to a fellow British officer and the confidence he expressed in the councils of the partisans co-existed in his own mind.

On an episodic level, 'what happened' appears to present few difficulties. The Second Sofia brigade commenced the march even more exhausted than Frank Thompson. They had been fighting in late April in the Kynstendal area. There had been continuous heavy fighting on the fourth to the sixth of May, with many losses and a rapid march from the seventh to the eleventh. On the eleventh and twelfth they had regrouped and collected their arms, and there had followed a council of

1   Letter to E.P. Thompson

81

war with Tempo, Apostolski and their staff, together with a delegation from the central committee in Sofia. The British Mission at this stage consisted of Major Thompson, Sergeant Scott, Sergeant 'Nick' Munro - a Canadian/Croat interpreter- and Sergeant Walker, the explosives expert. The Bulgarians included Vlado Trichkov - a bombastic orator, who made a great speech and crossed the border waving a tommy gun, Macho Ivanov, Vera Macheva, Georgi Chankov, Yordanka Chankova - 'sweet, mild-mannered, correct in her behaviour to every one' who became a friend of Frank's, Gocha Gopin - a lawyer, Dencho Znepolski, Balkanski, a wireless operator who had been dropped in and was in wireless contact with Dmitrov in Moscow, and about one hundred and eighty others, some of whom were new recruits.

Other partisans, including Dicha Petrov and a company from a Thracian watchtower were seconded to join them. They moved to the border, where they held a brief consultation, to which we will return later, and on the 17th they crossed into Bulgarian territory.

They went into the country, in Sergeant Scott's words. 'like a Sunday School outing', entering the villages of Govezhda and Dolgi Del quite openly. They went on in this way to the Kom mountains, reaching Zanage on the 21st May, passing through Lakatnik on the night of the 22nd and crossing the railway and the Iskur river in full daylight. They had hoped that by this time they would see some signs of the Chavdar brigade, but in fact that brigade had been destroyed by the third of May, and the people and animals had been removed from hills in the district. Guides who had been sent to warn the partisans had been killed at the Iskur river, so that they entered a district which, so far from offering support and reinforcements was riddled with ambushes.

By this time they were hungry and exhausted and had to rest. They conscripted two brothers from the local population who acted as unwilling guides and led them to a sheltered valley near Batoulia. The partisans, including those allocated sentry duty, fell asleep, and first one and then the other guide made his escape and went to warn the police and military. The brigade was surrounded and in the subsequent attack those who were not killed were scattered and broken up into small groups.

The mission was split - Munro and Walker were not seen again. One bunch of partisans in the rear, led by Znepolski, made their escape westward the way they had come. Thompson, Scott and the largest group headed forwards. They marched under conditions of incredible hardship. Several were wounded, incuding two of the girls among them, Bonka, the 'smallest partisan' who, although already a seasoned fighter was one of the youngest, barely out of her teens, and her friend Vessa who was a machine-gunner. Bonka had a stomach wound, Vessa had suffered from severe frostbite and was marching with septic and bleeding feet. Vlado Trichkov, the most senior of the partisans among them was also wounded. They had no maps or compass - the British soldiers, Thompson and Scott were appalled by the amateurishness and lack of provision of the partisan detatchment, but they were helpless to prevent the loss of direction which led the group in circles and too far south towards Sofia. They were eating what they could find in the countryside - snails and unripe fruit and little else. Bonka became too sick to follow them and was left in a shepherd's hut. Her later account provided some of the narrative of the group's movements. There were constant small skirmishes in which some partisans were killed; others deserted the band to find their own way into safer territory. On May 30th they reached a patch of woodland to the north of the village of Eleshina.

During the night of May 30/31 a small foraging party reached the village of Litakovo where they were given bread.

In spite of the fact that one of the sentries had disappeared during the night and might well have betrayed their position to the police, the partisans slept from sheer exhaustion.

On the morning of the 31st units of the Royal Bulgarian army and of the local police surrounded their position and in the afternoon began their attack. All attempts to break out were beaten back. A few found hiding places, including for a short time Frank Thompson and Sergeant Scott, but only two remained undiscovered. Thompson and Scott and those of the partisans who had not been killed were taken prisoner.

All the prisoners were taken to Eleshina where Scott and Thompson were questioned, first by the police and then more professionally by an army officer. Both gave only their name, rank and number. In the evening all the prisoners were driven to the village of Gorni Bogrov; the bodies of the partisans killed in the battle had been laid out in the public square at Eleshina, their heads had been severed and were taken to the headquarters at Gorni Bogrov, where they were displayed on pikes. Here all the prisoners were locked in the basement of the schoolroom where they joined the captured sentry and others who had been taken earlier. The prisoners were taken into the schoolyard and put on display before an audience of villagers who had been drummed up to view them. Attempts to stir up hostile demonstrations among the crowd were unsuccessful, however, indeed some clear sympathy was shown by villagers who handed bread and onions to the prisoners. The two women prisoners, Yordanka and Nicola had not been paraded in the schoolyard, but had been kept apart for special interrogation. Their screams were audible throughout the building during that night.

Thompson and Scott were taken out for interrogation by Bulgarian intelligence and by an officer of the Gestapo. Each was confronted by the SOE wireless set which Scott had buried further back, and both acknowledged their ownership of it. They were then shown a second - Russian - set of whose existence neither had known until that moment. Scott found his interrogators 'civilised' and was able to convince them that he had no knowledge of the second set. Thompson's interrogation was less gentlemanly. He had already avowed his communist sympathies and refused to explain his fluent Russian and Bulgarian. After these interviews, Scott was given medical attention and next day, 2nd June, taken by a German officer to Sofia.[1]

The remaining prisoners were taken out one by one to be executed, as were the peasants from Litakovo who had supplied them with bread. After two days Frank and the leading partisans were taken to Litakovo which had been chosen as the venue for a show trial.

The trial opened on 4th June in the village hall at Litakovo, before Colonel Manov as judge. Outside a dozen bodies of partisans were displayed in the village square, inside the hall was filled with villagers and soldiers. The calm bearing of the tall Englishman and the fact that he answered in their own language impressed the local people. Thompson again proclaimed his belief in communism and his solidarity with the other partisans in their battle against tyranny. An old

---

1   Scott was taken to Sofia where he was required to operate his wireless for the benefit of his captors. This eventuality had of course been foreseen and the agreed procedure alerted SOE headquarters at once. The signals were answered, and the longer the exchange was continued the better were Scott's chances of survival, as the Bulgarians became increasingly apprehensive of the approach of the Red Army and the withdrawal of the Germans. The Red Army crossed the frontier on 8th September 1944 and the next day Scott, wearing his RAF uniform was released in the centre of Sofia.

peasant woman stepped forward and declared herself on the side of the prisoners, and there seems to have been none of the hostility for which the organisers had hoped. The trial was brought to a rapid close and the prisoners were taken to a cliff above Litakovo where they were executed by a firing squad not made up of the local army or police but brought in especially from Sofia. Witnesses reported that the prisoners died with clenched fists and the partisan slogan 'Death to Fascism' on their lips. They were buried hurriedly in an unmarked grave.

In 1976 when the film makers came to England the director, Stancho Chausev, brought with him a small Roman silver coin which had been found sewn into Frank Thompson's tunic and had been removed half an hour after his death and presumably kept hidden. It was wrapped in a piece of paper with the single word Catullus written on it. Chausev gave the coin to Iris Murdoch.

It will be recalled that there had been a 'consultation' on the frontier, when Trifor Balkansky was over-ruled by Vlado Trichkov, Yordanka Chankova etc. But it is now necessary to clarify part of what took place in this consultation, for there was a hidden party to it.

The Bulgarian differed from the Yugoslav movement in being considerably more highly centralised. At first sight this might seem arguable, given that Tito centralised both political and military leadership in his own person. Nevertheless Tito, and the Yugoslav movement as a whole, successfully devolved authority and decision-making - for example to leaders such as Tempo and Apostolsky. This kind of devolution was never achieved within the Bulgarian Communist organisation. The Bulgarian was the oldest Communist Party in the Balkans and, through the status and activity of Dimitrov and Kolarov, was an exceedingly prestigious part of the Comintern, with a strong Moscow-based leadership. Boyan Bulgaranov, one of the Moscow-trained leaders, had negotiated with Tempo in Macedonia in 1943. Tempo found in him a 'bookish' Marxism and described him as

> One of the Comintern doctrinaires who considered that nothing had changed since the October Revolution, and that every revolution must unfold just like the October one; beginning with strikes, demonstrations and barricades and only after that organising an armed rising.[1]

Bulgaranov, therefore, and a weighty section of the Bulgarian Communist leadership wanted to organise not in the mountains but in the towns. In Tempo's view Bulgaranov 'loyally expressed Moscow's thinking' in that 'he judged the usefulness of [movements] not from the viewpoint of how far they contributed to the victory of socialism in that country, but of how far they facilitated the victory of the Red Army'. Tempo described a discussion he had with Bulgaranov about possible Bulgarian partisan actions. Bulgaranov said that they were working to get the whole of the army to come over to the allied side rather than organising small-scale armed resistance to the Germans. Tempo cut him short: 'I don't understand your policy, and even less the explanations which you are giving... You say you have, through your activity, prevented the departure of the Bulgarian army to the Eastern front...but it's come to the 'Yugoslav front' and replaced the German divisions which are sent to the Soviet front! In what then have you helped the Soviet army?...' I couldn't control myself and

1   Tempo typescript. Following quotations are all from this source. For his account of his meeting with Frank Thompson see *Struggle for the Balkans* pp. 315-321.

added a sarcastic question:

> How far do you wish to philosophise? Why don't you take
> rifles and hit the Germans? You ought to be concerned with
> real preparations so that you may strike the Germans...every
> day and every hour!' I expected a sharp reply, but not like the
> one that followed. Bulgaranov began with a threatening voice.
> 'You have insulted a great party...with a glorious past. One
> cannot speak thus of the party which organised the September
> rising...and which has given to the international workers'
> movement revolutionaries such as Dimitrov and Kolarov...
> You will answer for this...before the Comintern!'

The first change in the Bulgarian line occurred only in
early 1944. This involved the decision to establish an area of
free territory on the border, to send the headquarters of the
Bulgarian partisan movement there and to send recruits from
the interior there for training and organising. This was the
position which had been decided on in late April and early
May 1944. But a decisive message came to Kalna only on
about the tenth of May of that year. The instructions from the
Central Committee of the Bulgarian Communist Party were
brought from Sofia by Slavcho Trunski. 'He brought the news
that the centre of the uprising had been moved to Plovdiv,
where three members of the Politburo had gone - Isola
Drangoycheva, Dobri Terpshev and Anton Yugov.' Tempo's
account continues '...the politburo trio ordered Yordanka
Nikolova, Vlado Trichkov, Macho Ivanov and the second
Brigade to leave at once for Plovdiv'. More than this, they
appointed Dicho Petrov as commander of the Plovdev Zone.

The more I look at this, the more crazy it becomes. Here
were lines of command, grossly overstretched, issuing totally
unrealistic orders. Couriers took up to seven days to reach the
frontier - sometimes they were intercepted. No news had
reached the frontier of the defeat of the 'Chavdar' odred by the

88

third of May, a full week after it had occurred. These party leaders were no doubt courageous enough. They 'crossed from region to region, on foot, on horseback, by train or motor car... followed at every step by the enemy...' But this cannot excuse them from the accusation of acting in a doctrinaire and heavily over-centralised manner. To 'proclaim' from Sofia a 'free territory', to 'appoint' as commander the brave lieutenant of a former frontier post, Dicho Petrov, who was many hundreds of kilometres away appears to me as ideology and amateurism. How, moreover, had this fateful decision been reached? Here the evidence is not definitive. But for a number of reasons I am strongly inclined to accept the admittedly partial testimony of Vukmanovich (Tempo). It was not the politburo trio who conceived this plan - the plan came directly from Dimitrov in his Comintern office in Moscow. According to Tempo's account, Dimitrov had despatched a telegram demanding to know why the Bulgarian partisans had left Bulgaria, what they were doing on Yugoslav territory and how they thought they were going to take power in Bulgaria from a base in Yugoslavia?

If this is indeed the true account, a sour observation rises in one's mind. The Second Sofia brigade was destroyed by the doctrinaire chairborne instructions of Georgi Dimitrov - a hand had been reached out from Moscow to make use of that brave company as puppets in an ulterior national and revolutionary strategy.

It may or may not have been a crazy tactic and a crazy decision. I see it as crazy, amateurish and town-based, for it is possible to have envisaged the quiet infiltration of a partisan band into the countryside if it had been properly prepared and accompanied by reliable guides. Such a group accompanied by the British Mission to encourage and supervise arms drops could just possibly have succeeded and have provided a strong symbolic effect for potential resistance. I have suggested in the first lecture that Frank Thompson's instructions from Cairo gave him no option but to accept the plan and to go forward with Trichkov and Yordanka. I think the evidence suggests that he did go along with the plan and was preparing to organise air drops along the route. But there were further reasons, unknown to Thompson, why the plan was unworkable. The puppet-master's hand from Moscow was not the only one hovering over Kalna on May 12th.

If it is necessary to check back the Bulgarian lines of command and decision, it is also necessary to check back on those of the British. And we must check them back further than that curious amateurish outfit known as SOE Cairo.

On 24 February 1944 a directive was issued to Middle Eastern Forces. 'To force 133 - Re SOE/OSS operations in Bulgaria: Task to stimulate and encourage partisans with maximum possible support, having regard to forces available.'

The partisans were to be directed to create internal disorder which would compel recall of divisions garrisoning other Balkan territories, and 'lead ultimately to the overthrow of the present Bulgarian government by revolution'. The memo proposed that supplies of arms should be dropped to the Bulgarian partisans in a series of air sorties, 20 in February, 30 in March, 40 in April, 50 in May. It was signed simply 'Wilson'.[1]

This seems clear enough. If any author of this policy can be identified it was the British supreme commander ME, General 'Jumbo' Wilson, who had clearly declared - on 3rd

1   WO 204/1981, memo 24 February 1944. A report on Bulgaria in the same file dated 24 May 1944 suggests that they had in fact been able to make only 24 sorties between February and May 1944.

February - for a policy of 'giving the maximum possible assistance to all Bulgarian units or individuals who wish to fight GERMANS'. This military pressure was strong and continuing. SOE (Cairo) endorsed it. Tito and Tempo also endorsed and pressed for it.

Nevertheless, contrary advice came from the Foreign Office and from its advisers in the Middle East, including Lord Moyne. SOE (London) was also in opposition and perhaps OSS and the State Department. Various considerations influenced this alternative standpoint. Peace feelers were already being put out by this time to and from the Bulgarian government. There was the possibility of detaching the whole government and the army from the Axis 'as a going concern'. But there was as yet no common frontier between Bulgaria and the allies, so there was a case for lying low and waiting for an opportunity to mount an exercise which could achieve such a major break-through.

Early in March a memo was sent to General Wilson, questioning his policy. It suggested that in view of the peace feelers being put out by the Bulgarian government, Wilson's policy might well not bring the results 'which we wish to achieve if Bulgaria is genuinely willing to negotiate'. Were the government to lose control in Bulgaria it was likely that the Germans would take over the country.

> In these circumstances it will not be to our advantage either to secure the overthrow of a government which is willing to negotiate, or to embarrass its efforts to resist German occupation by creating conditions which will necessitate the employment of troops on internal security duties... From a purely military point of view it would suit our book better to have the whole country turn on the Germans as a going concern. We may hope to secure Bulgarian defection from Germany short of revolution, and the Fatherland Front partakes of the character rather of an instrument of pressure against the

present government than of the party with whom we hope ultimately to negotiate... Politically... it is clearly less embarrassing not to have to deal with a 'democratic' government in Bulgaria which would claim not only comradeship-in-arms with us in the anti-fascist struggle but also non-responsibility for the many and bloodthirsty crimes committed during the regime of their predecessors.[1]

Let us then resume the picture and see what we have. It is first of all of course, a great mistake to assume that states have one single coherent policy. Apart from the confusions of competing interests within any state, it is a matter of policy in all states to keep open several options. Mendacity is of the essence of statesmanship, and every state must have a left hand and a right. This was as true in 1944 of Russia as of Great Britain and the U.S.A. The Russians, with their right hand, played open diplomatic games with the Bulgarian government (and with the Allies) and with their left hand Dimitrov sent his signals to the partisans. The British policy was to use the partisans 'as an instrument of pressure' on the Bulgarian government, while hoping to bring that government across 'as a going concern'. There were also sub-plots which time does not allow me to pursue - Churchill's plan, for example, for a feint at a South East European offensive - perhaps still around at contingency level and resisted by the United States. But, as subsequent Foreign Office memos make clear the underlying thrust was - 'Bulgaria is being conquered, not liberated'. The British war aims after all included 'the preservation and eventual restoration of British and British

1   FO 371.43579 Steel to Howard 24/2/44. The main quotation is from this letter - other phrases come from correspondence in the same series.

Empire-owned property rights and interests.' More was at stake than simply diplomatic relations.

The aims and interests of the three parties involved, the Russians, the Allies and the partisans were incompatible. If Frank Thompson was on 'shifting sands', this was not only due to the inconsistencies of the partisans. A further influence also appears; where the British had hitherto been the senior partners on the allied side in the Balkans, now the beginnings of a new hegemony were revealing themselves. The Bulgarian government was increasingly putting out feelers not to Great Britain but to the United States, via Istanbul. On the twenty-first of April, when Frank was writing his last letter from Tergoviste, the United States consul in Istanbul reported new approaches from the Bulgarian government:

> The Bulgarians are aware that decisive events for their country are at hand. Our conviction is that if the moderate and governing classes can not take immediate steps to get Bulgaria out of the war there will be a Communist and pro-Soviet rising in some form as soon as the Soviet Armies approach the Bulgarian frontier... While the Bulgarians are willing to treat with the Americans they are loath to treat with the British...[1]

On *the same day* SAC (Algiers) reached out and put the Balkans operations 'on hold'. There were to be no further actions outside Yugoslavia and Albania without prior approval. The decision taken in February to build up the Bulgarian partisan movement was reversed and it was laid down that future supplies should be limited to the maintenance of existing commitments and for intelligence purposes only.

1   Foreign Relations of the UP Washington 1965, Vol 111, 1944. pp. 321-2, (April 21).

No inkling of this change of policy went out to the field. At SOE Cairo the head of that section (Sweet-Escott) was away. What, anyway, was an 'existing commitment'? For several weeks SOE prevaricated and questioned. Signals went back and forth between Cairo and Algiers. SAC confirmed this on 10th of May, reconfirmed it on 20th May.

If Dimitrov's was the hand behind the Sofia partisan headquarters, the hand behind SAC was, most probably, that of Winston Churchill. Churchill's very sharp and decisive turn against EAM has been discussed by others[1] and the occasion for his latest explosion was not Bulgaria but a small incident of SOE bungling in Roumania. On the fourth of May he sent a memo to Eden saying 'that it was essential to face the brute issues between us and the Soviet government which are developing in Italy, in Roumania, in Bulgaria, in Yugoslavia and above all in Greece... are we going to acquiesce in the Communization of the Balkans and perhaps of Italy...' In all these areas he saw 'a Communist influence and invasion' - and, three days later 'It does seem to me that SOE barges in in an ignorant manner into all sorts of delicate situations. They were originally responsible for building up the nest of cockatrices for EAM in Greece...' Churchill was at this stage 'willing to discuss' with Eden the breaking up of SOE and its placing under military and Foreign Office control.

This, then, was not the most favourable situation for any British mission to enter Bulgaria. Although no one had bothered to inform it, the action, even if successful, would have been in defiance of SAC instructions and all sorties had been placed 'on hold'. It was even less favourable for a

1   Elizabeth Barker, *British Policy in SE Europe* Ch. 13 and for the Roumanian episode Ch. 18.

mission commanded by an officer known to be a communist. On the sixth of April Winston Churchill had written to the British ambassador in Algiers - 'I suppose you realise that we are weeding out remorselessly every single known Communist from all our secret organisations...',[1] and, in a minute of the thirteenth of April, 'We are purging all our secret establishments of Communists because we know they owe no allegiance to us or our cause and will always betray secrets to the Soviet, even while we are working together...'[2]

The British mission which 'galloped' off from Kalna on the twelfth of May had already, in effect, been disowned in its rear. It was not so much in the hands of a puppet master as totally discarded.

Let us now spend some moments in reflection. I will say only a little about the most manifest theme - the origins and issues of the Cold War. Every one has his or her own thoughts and meditations on this. I want to add only a little more material for meditation, and will make only three observations.

Firstly, in much western historiography Churchill has been applauded for his turn - a turn actively supported by elements in OSS and by the U.S. State Department. But to agree with Churchill that Russia was engaged in a drive for power in South Eastern Europe need not bring us to his conclusions. The response to this situation need not have been the defence of old western interests and a covert alliance with what were called 'the governing and moderate classes'. How 'moderate' were these classes in Bulgaria, how moderate had

1   Letter to Ambassador in Algiers, 6 April 1944, Avon papers, University Birmingham SOE/44/17
2   Minute of 13 April 1944, in Winston S. Churchill, *Closing the Ring* p.542

been their government? An OSS Report discussed atrocities committed by the Bulgarian authorities against captured partisans. It is difficult to agree with a description of those who raped Yordanka before they killed her as 'moderate'. The underlying notion in this tradition of historiography is that it was somehow 'unfair' that partisans in the Balkans (or, for that matter, in Italy) should 'take advantage of the war' to effect revolutionary changes in the property statutes and the state organisations of their countries. They should have allowed themselves to be used loyally as 'instruments of pressure', thereby enabling the Western allies to defeat the German antagonist and then to restore the old order - the monarchy, the army, the police, the property statutes 'as a going concern'. I don't know why historians on this side of the Atlantic should be quite so confident about this attitude. I have heard - but perhaps this is only a myth - that revolutions and civil wars have occurred here also. In Europe, by contrast, the peasants and the poor had 'loyally' endured for centuries the demands of authoritarian masters. For most of Europe the first World War had been the dominating experience - their children had been sent out to death in myriads by their masters so that the old order could be restored. Why should another generation of the rural and urban poor young men and women, go out and face torture and death for Mr Churchill or General Donovan, but not for causes of their own?

But secondly, to say that the partisan commitment to social revolution was open and honourable is not to go on and assent to the Great Power strategies of the Soviet Union, or to those of the Comintern or of Dimitrov. There is substantial evidence that the Soviet state disliked the self-activating revolutionary democracy of the partisan movement only a little less than did the western allies. When Soviet forces entered Bulgaria in September 1944 they acted rapidly to bring the partisan areas under control and to reinstate the army as 'a going concern'. The Russian state had, indeed, by 1944 long lost any taste for revolutionary movements except as 'instruments of pressure.' They were happy to trade the fate of EAM into the hands of Churchill and their suspicion of the Yugoslav movement long preceded the Cominform anathema. For revolutionary movements supported by military missions from the west they had an active dislike.

My third point then is therefore clear. There were the strongest reasons of state - of *both* states - why the British mission, and its leader, Frank Thompson, in particular were seen to be expendable. The question remains, was Frank Thompson so expended? It is here that we cannot expect the sources to reveal any part of the truth. There is clear evidence, even in those portions of the British records which have been released, of very heavy and specific weeding between March and June 1944. What is partially revealed (from scraps which it would be tedious to detail) is that the right hand of the Western alliance was active in these months - all through that time peace feelers were being met, via Ankara and the U.S.A. What the Bulgarian authorities wanted, in return for a promise to switch allegiance at an opportune moment, was an end to Western stimulation of partisan and subversive activities. What discussions went on, what promises were made, we cannot say. But the period between Frank's capture on 31st May and his execution on 5th June was a substantial one. The decision to shoot him was not taken by a local police captain. Martial law was indeed in force, but the order for this action came from a higher authority. Thompson's notebooks were seized and a translator was interrogated about their contents before the Regency Council. On the first of June, moreover, a new administration under Bogrianov came to power. At that point in the war it seems inconceivable that the authorities would have ordered the execution of a British officer in uniform if some gesture or signal had not passed which

97

offered them some license. Somebody winked.

I cannot at this time prove that this was so. It may be that eventually Bulgarian or even United States sources will throw more light on the question. I can only show that Claridges was an embarrassment to the British and that it has always remained so. I suspect that SOE Cairo received a sharp reproof for allowing it to go ahead, hence the continued prevarication from that source about the order to go into Bulgaria. A Foreign Office memo of August speaks in tones of disdain. The Bulgarian partisans are described as being in a high proportion 'traditional Bulgarian brigands'. As to British support for them, it was held that 'the risking of the lives of spirited young officers, not to speak of arms deliveries to most undesirable elements are not worth the candle...'

Is this then to be our judgement also - that the whole episode was 'not worth the candle'? It is in a sense the easiest judgement to make -

> The tall unwounded leader
> Of doomed companions, all
> Whose voices in the rocks
> Are now perpetual.
> Fighters for no one's sake
> Who died beyond the border.[1]

I find this too easy. Yet I find any other conclusion difficult. The first and enduring meaning of the episode I find in its lesson of the total mendacity of states: the manipulation and cancellation of the motives of individuals within the amoral

1   These lines from W.H. Auden's *Poems* (1941) were cited by Frank in a letter home to Edward in 1941. The title Edward gave to this series of lectures obviously derives partly from these lines.

interests of collectivities.

Yet we have to reach towards other conclusions also. These conclusions may not be the same for you as for me, for I have a more personal demand for understanding.

My brother's own conclusions will never be known. I can suppose one of these with confidence. He would have resented this special treatment of his own part, the casting of him as hero. He endured a fate shared by his British colleagues Walker and Munro, and by his friends and comrades, Trichkov, Yordanka, Gorcha Gopin. The shattered bodies of these friends were dumped in the square at Litakovo and their decapitated heads leered down from stakes. He cannot have expected, nor even much desired, an exception from this common fate by virtue of the privilege of British nationality.

For the rest, he had adequate time for reflection in the last few days at Litakovo. The body, after these intense marches and privations, was recuperating.

His reflections in some part will have been bitter. It was a hard death to face, not in the press and bewilderment of battle, but after utter disaster, due, he must have known, at least in part to the self-inflicted blunders of his own party. He had seen the death of his comrades, the failure of popular support, and now faced long days in which to reflect upon all this and upon his own departing life.

Yet this death was one which he had long anticipated - which he had even gone out to meet - ' A democrat' he wrote in one of his last letters home,

has a great advantage over the people whom he is fighting. Even his death is, in a sense, creative. When a democrat dies - that is, a man who has shown...by word and action that he cares more than anything for democratic freedom - then one, or ten, or a hundred new ones are created by his example; one, or ten, or a hundred existing ones are strengthened in their resolve. When a fascist dies the effect on his confederates is the reverse. Only in the most confused and darkest periods of history does this not appear to be the case.

But we were already moving, then, into one such 'confused and dark moment of history'.

It is clear enough, surely, from my last lecture and this, that Frank Thompson's commitment to any cause of 'Communism' represented by the Soviet Union or the Comintern would scarcely have lasted another three years - perhaps as far as the Kostov trial?[1] It would certainly not have lasted as long as my own.

What 'meaning', in any case, can one attribute to any historical event? Is not history always a record of the supercession and cancellation of individual meanings and motives in the sum which makes up historical process? And is not process itself devoid of all inherent significance, value-free, to which we may then if we so wish, bring attributions of value from outside?

In my own writings on history and theory I have assented to this position. But I have gone on to add that it is we, in the present, who must always give meaning to that inert and finished past. For history is forever unresolved, it remains as a field of unfinished possibilities, it lies behind us with all its contradictions of motives and cancelled intentions and we - acting in the present - reach back, refuse some possibilities and select and further others. We endorse some values of the past, we refuse others.

In these perspectives I will argue that the meaning of that journey across a frontier and of that death at Litakovo remains unresolved. For thirty and more years the resolution has

1   *The Trial of Traicho Kostov and his Group* [for treason, espionage and betrayal of the fatherland] Sofia 1949.

100

appeared to be one of betrayal and cynicism -

> Fighters for no one's sake
> Who died beyond the border.

Yet alternative possibilities remain. They have not been utterly cancelled.

One set of possibilities was embodied in the values of comradeship; the comradeship of that company of marchers and also perhaps in the genuine warmth felt by simple Bulgarian peasants and workers at the internationalist pledge given by the British presence in their own adversity. This was voiced at the time. Dencho Znepolski wrote of Frank:

> He was very much attached to the people, and showed great interest in the peasant life. He showed a happy and kind character, both when he spoke Bulgarian and when he danced the Bulgarian national dances. It was difficult to tell he was a foreigner. He got used to everything, he was hungry with the rest of us, had to fight the second enemy of the partisans - the lice - just as everybody else did. This is what binds people together in the struggle against Fascism. This made the Bulgarian partisans and the Bulgarian people feel Thompson close to their hearts...

Writing to Frank's parents in November 1944, Anthony Strachey recalled speaking to Bulgarian partisan leaders in the months after his death. One partisan leader who was himself killed shortly afterwards, said 'Yes, he was a good man, he shared our hardships, he understood our problems and he even learnt our songs'. 'This', Strachey commented, 'is no small tribute from a vital unruly people very suspicious of all foreigners, especially the British.' This sense survives still and with warmth. Sometimes it appears in popular myth, sometimes in the work of a new, critical and disenchanted generation of Bulgarian scholars.

Internationalism can never be created only by rhetoric and diplomatic protocol. It requires another kind of symbolism and it demands proofs in the form of sacrifices. The other, and coincident, possibilities in the story were those which Frank Thompson expressed repeatedly in his letters, which concerned new possibilities of European democracy. He wrote about this in his diary of 25th February 1943:

> ...what a pleasant prospect it raises! How wonderful it would be to call Europe one's fatherland, and think of Krakov, Munich, Rome, Arles, Madrid as one's own cities! I am not yet educated to a broader nationalism, but for a United States of Europe I could feel a patriotism far transcending my love for England. Differences between European peoples, though great, are not fundamental. What differences there are serve only to make people mutually more attractive. Not only is this Union the only alternative to disaster. It is immeasurably more agreeable than any way of life we have known to date.

On Christmas day of the same year he wrote in a letter to his brother:

> There is a spirit abroad in Europe which is finer and braver than anything that tired continent has known for centuries, and which cannot be withstood. You can, if you like, think of it in terms of politics, but it is broader and more generous than any dogma. It is the confident will of whole peoples who have known the utmost humiliation and suffering and have triumphed over it, to build their own life once and for all... There is a marvellous opportunity before us - and all that is required from Britain, America and the U.S.S.R. is imagination, help and sympathy...

Nothing now reads as a sicker epitaph for the second world war than that. It was a young man's illusion, cancelled utterly within a few years by the oncoming Cold War.

Yet historians know that every great historical impulse is

always preceded many decades before, by premonitions which appear to the actors as abject failures. I am myself not sanguine: I anticipate that the Cold War will - and in this generation - work out to its terminus. Yet if an alternative logic could be found, it could only be in a renewal of that closed field of possibility. A new generation would have to arise which would repudiate the whole set of post-war betrayals - the Rajk and Slansky and Kostov trials and all that they stood for, the arrest of democratic advance and the polarisation of wealth and power in the West, the barbaric symbolic vocabulary of exterminist missiles, and would turn back again to the alternative possibilities and intentions of that brief high-spirited moment of democratic anti-fascist alliance. For although there are many lies about the past, some of which I have tried to nail in these lectures - this is not, I think, one of them.

Fascism provoked a determination to resist and a spirit of sacrifice. Above all, in the young resisters there was a shared faith and an internationalist fellowship - pledged in many cases to the end of life - which tower above the spiritual poverty of the present. This moment remains as a symbol of the possible. Yet it was a possible generated only in the extremity of war and repression.

Are such resources of the spirit only to be summoned out of war? Is it even possible to conceive of such a spirit in Europe - or anywhere in the world - in advance of a war which, if it comes, will leave no resisters and nothing except missiles to resist? This is not a question which we can ask of history. It is, this time, a question which history asks of us.

Epilogue

Litakovo, Bulgaria 10th June 1994

A DAY or two after the ceremonies which marked the fiftieth anniversary of the re-invasion of France by Allied forces, another, smaller, ceremony of remembrance was held at the other end of Europe near the small village of Litakovo in Western Bulgaria.

This ceremony also marked a fiftieth anniversary, that of the execution of a band of Bulgarian partisans, survivors of the Second Sofia Liberation Brigade, their British liaison officer, Major Frank Thompson and villagers from Litakovo who had given them help. The bodies of those executed had originally been buried in a common grave in the village square, but had later been removed to graves surrounding the memorial erected on a small hill near the village to mark the twenty-fifth anniversary of their execution.

The simple and moving ceremony began with an address of welcome given by His Excellency the British Ambassador, Mr Richard Thomas. The Defence Attache, Colonel Robert Pearson, then read a short account of the events leading up to the execution and a brief personal history of Major Thompson with a Bulgarian translation read by Lieutenant Colonel Ivan Milanov of the Bulgarian army. English and Bulgarian versions of the poems 'Sharing' by Christo Botev and 'An Epitaph for my Friends' (Polliticii Meliora) by Frank Thompson were read by members of the Embassy staff.

Wreaths were laid on the memorial obelisk by the British Ambassador and the Defence Attache on behalf of the British Government and Armed Forces, and by Major General Lyubomir Vassilev, Commander First Army, on behalf of the Bulgarian Armed Forces. Last Post and Reveille were played by the Band of Sofia Garrison while the guard of honour provided by the Botevgrad Garrison presented arms.

This was followed by the two national anthems. After the formal ceremony flowers were laid on individual graves by many of those attending.

In addition to members of the British Embassy and the Bulgarian Ministry of Defence, there were numbers of people from the village of Litakovo, many of whom had been children and innocent observers of the events of June 1944. Frank Thompson's sister-in-law and his two nephews were also present.

The ceremony was intensely moving and served to remind us all of the resistance to tyranny and autocracy which was to be found in all parts of the continent in those dark years.

The justice and freedom for which the partisans and their helpers died may not have been available to all in the intervening years but we can still see the defeat of Fascism and the victory of the Allies as the turning point in opening the way for a better and freer world. We met to honour the courage and sacrifice of the partisans and the British liaison officer who served and died with them who did not live to see the final victory.

Dorothy Thompson

A Note on Sources

THE lecture scripts on which this book is based were prepared by Edward for oral delivery, and did not contain detailed footnotes. Where possible the source of specific quotations has now been indicated, but not more general sources for other types of statement or opinion.

There is now quite a considerable literature about the partisan warfare in the Balkans. Edward read everything that was published in English before he wrote this account, but listed here are only those books which actually refer to the Bulgarian episode or to Frank Thompson himself. For material published in Bulgarian or in Serbo Croat, he obtained working translations of sections which referred to the partisans and in particular of course to the British mission. There was therefore among his notes a substantial batch of typescript translations which included reminiscences especially produced by Generals Tempo and Apostolski, and translations from those of the books listed below which have not been translated.

Oral and Manuscript sources

Much of the material from which his narrative has been constructed was given by contemporaries of Frank in the army or SOE. Edward was particularly grateful for this help which often entailed the recall of painful memories and invariably the expenditure of time and trouble. I hope that all those who helped are mentioned in the acknowledgements, but apologise sincerely to any who may have been omitted.

Manuscript material is mostly from papers in the possession of the Thompson family. These papers will go to the Bodleian library in the not too distant future, but at present they are not calendered or catalogued in any way. Among them are pretty well every letter written by Frank to his parents since his earliest schooldays and wartime letters to his brother and to some of his friends, as well as his own journals, again in many cases going back into his schooldays but continued throughout most of his time in the army. I have indicated the date of letters and journal entries, and in some cases the person to whom the letter was addressed. Where no name is given the letters were to his family, often addressed to 'Dear Folks' and intended for parents and brother.

Official documentation of the war in the Balkans is still very thin. Although some material was released in the 1970s under the thirty year rule for public records, sections of government papers, including the Prime Minister's papers relating to Bulgaria in the later years of the war have been extensively weeded. More may still be learnt if papers are released after further years of secrecy. The papers of SOE seem to be a kind of private archive to which only selected friends and relations of the archivists are given access. Thus some accounts have been published which refer to the Bulgarian mission, but Edward was not himself allowed access to the documents on which these were based. Where official documents of any kind have been quoted, series and folio numbers are given.

Another obvious source of information would be the official papers of the Bulgarian government - both those of the pre-1944 administration and of the Communist governments which followed. Penetration of Bulgarian archives was, when

108

these lectures were written, impossible for British historians, and even the accounts which were published by the Communist government give no reference for sources, and indeed in some cases contain material which patently goes against the information for which we have other documentation. It may be however that there is documentation still in these archives which will eventually add to the picture.The only primary material from Bulgaria which was used here was the English translation of the transcript of the trial of Traicho Kostov, Sofia 1949. For the other Bulgarian material listed below, we obtained translations of passages which appeared to refer to Frank Thompson or his mission.

When these lectures were being prepared, the memoirs of Tempo (General S. Vukmanovich) had not been published in English. Tempo gave an account of his relations with Frank Thompson to Edward, and both he and his wartime associate, Apostolski, answered questions by correspondence. Edward also had a translation of the relevant passages from the Yugoslav edition of Tempo's memoirs. In the list below the English edition is given, but the extracts in the text may not always correspond in pagination or exact translation, since they are taken from the typescript.

Published material

The main published source for Frank Thompson's own writing is the collection made by his mother and his brother and published in 1947 and 1948. Some of Frank's poems were reprinted in school magazines, and one or two others have appeared in anthologies of poems from the Second World War. One poem 'Pollitici Meliora' was read at the broadcast ceremony commemorating the end of the war in Europe and also at that which commemorated the end of the war itself. I have not listed these separately as they are printed in the collection below.

E.P. Thompson and T.J. Thompson (eds), *There is a Spirit in Europe* (London: Victor Gollancz, 1947, 2nd edn, 1948).

A collection of letters, diaries, poems and other writings together with the best account of the Bulgarian expedition it was possible to give at that time.

There are three later accounts of the Bulgarian expedition:

Stowers Johnson, *Agents Extraordinary* (London: Robert Hale, 1975).

Fred Inglis, *The Cruel Peace* (New York: Basic Books 1991). Ch.,1 pp. 3 - 31. [Inglis had read the manuscript of Edward's lectures when he wrote this chapter]

Slavcho Trunski, *Grateful Bulgaria* (Sofia: 1979). [Contains reminiscences of partisans who were still living in the '70s].

Short list of other works in English:

The Trial of Traicho Kostov and his Group, (Sofia: 1949).

Bickham Sweet-Escott, *Baker Street Irregular* (London: Methuen, 1965).

Elisabeth Barker, *British Policy in South-East Europe in the Second World War* (London: Macmillan 1976).

M.R.D.Foot, *Resistance* (London: Eyre Methuen, 1976).

Stoyan Rachev, *Anglo-Bulgarian Relations during the Second World War (1939-1944)* (Sofia: Sofia Press, 1981).

Freeman Dyson, *Disturbing the Universe* (New York: Harper Row, 1979).

David Stafford, *Britain and European Resistance* (London: Macmillan, 1980).

Svetozar Vukmanovich [General Tempo], *Struggle for the Balkans* (Belgrade: 1980; London: Merlin 1990).

Philip Warner, *Phantom* (London: William Kimber 1982)

Works in Bulgarian:

Trifon Balkanski, *Nashite Partizanski Patishta* 2nd edn, (Sofia: 1967).

Slavcho Trunski, *Neotdavna*, 4th edn, (Sofia: 1974)

Orlin Vasilev, *Vaorazhenata Saprovitiva Sreshtu Fashizma v Balgariya, 1923-1944* (Sofia: 1946; preface by Traicho Kostov).

Kiril Markov-Slatan *V Boy Posleden* (Sofia: 1966).